MY CHILD IS NOT MISSING

MY CHILD IS NOT MISSING

A PARENTS' GUIDEBOOK
FOR THE PREVENTION AND
RECOVERY OF MISSING CHILDREN

COMPILED BY

CHILD SAFE PRODUCTS, INC.

Beverly Huttinger, Writer
John Anderson, Researcher

MY CHILD IS NOT MISSING
Compiled by Child Safe Products, Inc.

Copyright 1984/All rights reserved
Child Safe Products, Inc.
Second Printing

Produced by Ratzlaff & Wright Associates
Published by Child Safe Products, Inc.
449 N. University Drive
Plantation, Florida 33324

Library of Congress:
Card Catalogue No.: 84-71008

Trade Softback Edition
ISBN: 0-917461-00-2
Retail Price $12.95

Printed in the United States of America

DEDICATION

It is our fervent hope that missing children everywhere can be reunited with the families who wait for them, that they can grow up to raise their children in a country that is truly free.

We pray that this program will play a part in solving one of the most distressing problems this country has ever faced and in making America once again a safe place for our children.

With families and loved ones, we too grieve for the children who are still missing. It is to them that we dedicate this book.

ACKNOWLEDGMENTS

This book is based, for the most part, upon information provided by people whose lives have been touched by the agony of a missing child — people who gave graciously of their time and thought to reflect upon painful experiences in the hope that others might be spared.

We especially thank Julie and Stanley Patz, parents of Etan Patz; Gloria Yerkovich and the staff of Child Find, Inc., New Paltz, N.Y.; James De Gray, founder of James De Gray Foundation for Missing Children, Tampa, Florida; Betty DiNova of Dee Scofield Awareness Program, Tampa, Florida; Ivana DiNova, founder of Missing Children's Help Center, Tampa, Florida; Lt. Eric Krantz of the Blairstown, New Jersey Police Department; Bill Bardenwerper of the Louisville-Jefferson County Joint Task Force; the F.B.I. in Washington, D.C. and Fort Lauderdale, Florida. To the many, many others whose words, efforts, and concerns stimulated the preparation of this book, we again extend our heartfelt love.

TABLE OF CONTENTS

CHAPTER I

INTRODUCTION

*Since children often cannot speak out,
others must speak out for them.*

Ann Landers

THE CHILLING REALITY

"My child is missing . . ."
probably one of the most frightening realizations a parent can experience.

The statistics are grim.

Every year in the United States, 50,000 children, above and beyond those abducted by disputing parents, simply disappear, often without a clue. Of this number 4,500 are found alive, but badly molested; 33,000 are found dead. Each year 12,500 children are added to the "still missing" rolls.

But this appalling figure accounts for only one-third of the total. Over twice as many children are taken by their own parents, many of whom are vindictive and unstable. Parental abduction, once considered a harmless domestic situation, has burgeoned into a national disgrace, leaving heartbreak in its wake.

A half century ago, "getting lost" seldom ended in tragedy. The thought of a child in danger always prodded a concerned citizenry into immediate action. In nearly all cases the child was returned to his parents alive and unharmed.

A notable exception was the case of 20-month-old Charles A. Lindbergh, Jr. In March, 1932, five years after his father became a national hero by his famous transAtlantic crossing, Charles Jr. was discovered missing from his crib. An awkwardly penciled note, demanding a $50,000 ransom, was left in the baby's room, clearly indicating a kidnapping.

The crime shocked the nation. For months, front page headlines kept the public informed of the smallest details of the investigation. When the child's body was discovered in the New Jersey woods two months later, the entire nation felt as if it had suffered a personal loss.

An unidentified child about a year-old, lies wrapped in a a
jacket on a back door stoop in Boston's Dorchester section.
According to police, the baby boy was left outside the home
as a result of a parental disagreement.

Today a lost child is commonplace; newspapers rarely carry the story at all. Overburdened police forces often can make only feeble efforts at recovery. To outsiders, the shock value is lost. But to parents and loved ones, it is a cruel reality.

Stan Patz, whose son Etan disappeared in 1979, explains, "Child snatching, kidnapping and the ugly things that happen to these kids are so horrendous that people refuse to deal with them." But the growing number of tragic incidents has forced Americans to examine the problem and search for a solution. We can no longer evade the responsibility of taking a good, hard look at what happens to missing children.

Tara Burke of San Francisco was one of them.

In 1982, two-year-old Tara was abducted by two men who kept her for their own sadistic sexual pleasure. For ten and one-half months, she was held chained and naked in a filthy van. In exchange for grubby meals, she was forced to perform lewd acts that no two-year-old could possibly understand.

Fortunately for Tara and her family, her case had a happy ending. An 11-year-old boy who had also been held by the men managed to escape and lead the police to Tara. In the care of a wise and loving family, she now shows every sign of recovering from her ordeal.

But in cases like this, where a child has been missing for several months or longer, happy endings are rare. More typical are heartbreak and tragedy, as in the following cases:

In Ocala, Florida, 12-year-old Dee Scofield was allegedly seen two hours after her disappearance in July of 1976 from a grocery store. She was in the back of a van and seemed to be forming the word "help" with her lips. Although several other alleged sightings have been reported, Dee has never been found.

In Utah, near Hill Air Force Base, Elaine Runyon watched Rachael, her three-year-old daughter, as she went to play in a park about ten feet away from her backyard fence. Because of the fence, Rachael left her sight for a few minutes. In those few minutes she disappeared. A month later, in an isolated area, police found her body.

On September 6, 1981, two-and-a-half-year-old Ryan Burton was abducted from her bed as she slept in Breckenridge, Texas. She is still missing.

Rosemary Murphy, a 26-year-old divorcee, spent two years and almost $35,000 to recover her son Chad, who was literally taken from her arms—by his own father. When she finally found him, he did not recognize her and did not even know his real name.

In Orlando, Florida, in 1983, two 14-year-old girls, Barbara Ann Byer and Angelica Jean Lavallee, ran away from home, hitching a ride with two men they did not know. Six months later, one of the men led police to Barbara Ann's skeletal remains and told them that his companion had murdered her. Angelica is still missing.

It is reassuring to know that most lost children are found and returned to loving arms within the first few hours after the report of their disappearance. Toddlers wander away to look for the home of a friend or grandparent, or to follow a dog or cat behind hedges into neighboring yards. Youngsters stop off at their friends' homes after school and lose track of time playing or watching TV, unmindful of the worries and fears building up in the hearts of those waiting for them at home. Children old enough to know better forget to tell about after-school meetings or practice, or, thoughtless and independent, go off with friends to video game rooms without letting anyone know.

But more and more children are not returning. The

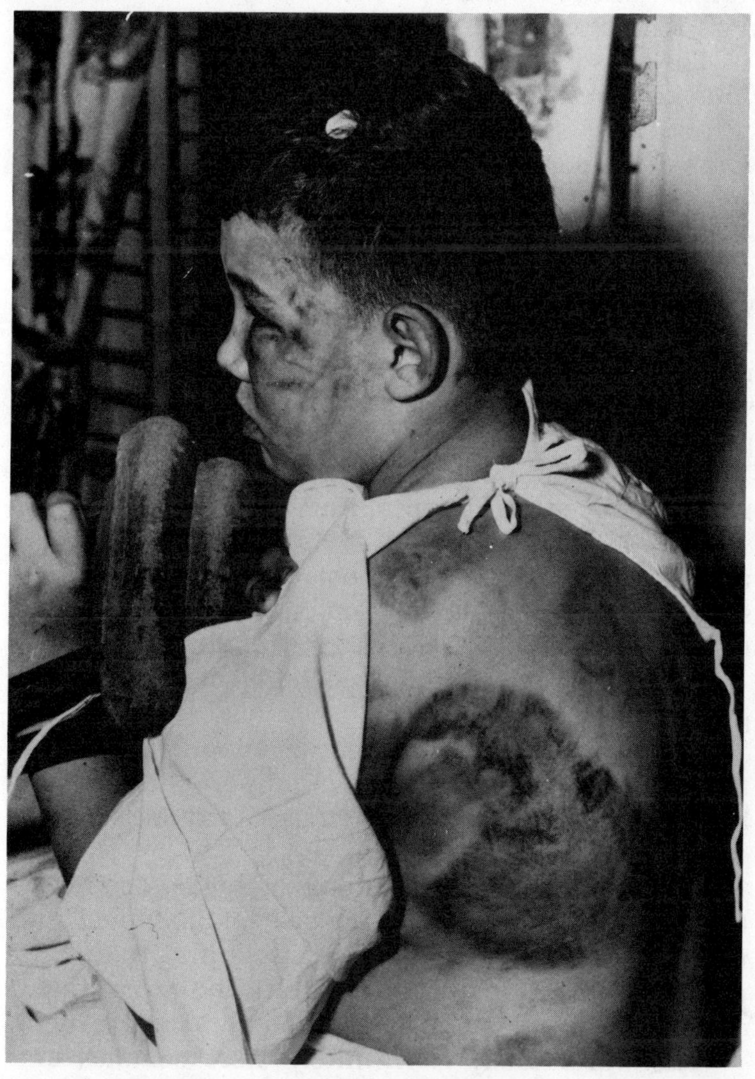

Beaten child, Ronnie Deere, age 9, sits on a hospital bed in Wichita, Kansas, showing some of the bruises he received in a beating while visiting relatives.

number of those found dead, or savagely molested, or not found at all continues to rise at an alarming rate.

The reasons for their disappearance vary tremendously and reflect the instability of unsettled times in a "throwaway" society. Many of these children are unwanted . . . some literally tossed out of the door by frustrated parents no longer able to cope with economic setbacks, emotional disturbances, or the irrational, often drug-related, behavior of their offspring. Some youngsters leave of their own accord, choosing an unknown life on the streets over intolerable conditions, real or imagined, at home. In Fort Lauderdale, one 15-year-old told a reporter, "I didn't run away; I walked. My parents didn't care."

Many other children go with parents, or other relatives, or acquaintances. And others are taken by strangers —strangers with twisted minds who, for reasons unfathomable to most of us, find deranged satisfaction in the torture, mental anguish, and in many cases cold-blooded murder of children.

Besides the very real possibility of murder, the parents of a missing child must also live with the abhorrent realities of black market adoptions, pseudo-religious cults, white slavery, child pornography, and homosexual and prostitution rings . . . any one of which could claim their child.

Dealing in children has taken on epidemic proportions. It is not uncommon today for abducted and runaway children to be bought, sold and traded for practices once termed unthinkable. The exploiting of children for profit has become a million-dollar business.

The world today is infinitely more complex and dangerous than it was a generation ago. While the problem of missing children was not unknown, it was something that most people didn't have to think about.

But with tragedy occurring on every side, no parent can any longer afford to believe that it only happens to other people. No truly concerned parent dares to leave the safety of his child to chance.

Much of a child's world today is strange, unfamiliar and often hostile. Just as an adult would prepare himself for a journey into unfamiliar territory, today's child must be oriented and equipped to handle himself in a complex environment. A youngster moving to a new city or into a new neighborhood, a child going to school for the first time, or entering a new school, a toddler growing into a wider world, or a half-child, half-adult groping to find himself — needs preparation to meet the unexpected hazards of the new or larger world he is entering.

With this preparation, many cases of missing children would have been preventable. And this is the greatest tragedy of all—the needlessness of the suffering and agony of both children and their parents.

This is what our book is all about—the prevention of the tragedy of lost children by planning and preparing to meet the unexpected. And for those whose children are already missing, we offer hope for recovery—positive steps that can be taken to end the nightmare of waiting and hoping.

Police carry the body of a child found in Atlanta, Georgia, 1980. The victim appeared to be 11 or 12 years old.

CHAPTER II

THE CHILD ABDUCTORS

*In a secular age, children have
become the last sacred objects.*

Joseph Epstein

THE UNKNOWN PROFILE

What does a kidnapper look like . . . or act like? Unfortunately, pretty much like everyone else. Why would anyone want to take someone else's child? There is a rather loosely defined "profile" of a kidnapper. Usually he's someone who's around children a lot, often preferring their company to that of adults. He may feel sexually inadequate with adults and more comfortable with children. He might have a history of child abductions. But in many cases he has shown no other criminal behavior or any other apparent psychotic quirks. His facial expressions, mannerisms and movements reveal nothing to set him apart. Go to a shopping mall, a crowded beach or a baseball game and try to pick out the kidnappers. You would more than likely end up accusing someone whose greatest crime has been a traffic violation, while the real culprits would slip unnoticed through your fingers.

The abductor or molester of children fits no pattern. He is of no particular age, race, occupation, nationality or sex. In most cases, he is someone the child knows. Certainly the most publicized cases of abduction have been by strangers. Your child should be told, just as you probably were when you were a child, not to talk to strangers or accept gifts, money or rides from them.

But society's stereotype of the legendary character in the big car and raincoat, offering candy to unsuspecting school children, is dangerously misleading. Many parents believe their children will be safe if they simply do not talk to strangers. In the great majority of child abductions, however, 89% by one count, the abductor was someone **known** to the child.

Newsweek magazine has stated that one out of ten children is sexually abused each year, and only a small

F.B.I. agents accompany an unidentified kidnapping suspect after his capture in a Boston downtown parking garage.

percentage by strangers. Much more often it is by someone the child trusts — a friend of a parent, an aunt or uncle, a school custodian, a maintenance or recreation worker at a park or playground, even a minister or teacher. And probably the most devastating experience of all occurs when a child is molested by his own parent, a far from uncommon event today.

THE PARENT

The American Bar Association Journal estimates that in one out of ten divorces an abduction results, totalling possibly 100,000 or more kidnappings a year.

A harmless situation? Emphatically not. Parental abduction can be devastating for the parent with legal custody who may live for years with the knowledge that the child is probably alive—somewhere. And it can be equally devastating for the child, who very often has to live with a parent who is running from the law and clearly has other motives than the child's welfare.

On December 20, 1974, Gloria and Ray Yerkovich, now directors of Child Find, Inc., reluctantly allowed Franklin Pierce, the father of Gloria's daughter, Joanna, to take the child for a weekend visit. It was in compliance with a court order. "As soon as they left," Gloria recalls, "I was filled with dread. I could still see her kicking and hear her screaming; I think she was afraid she wasn't coming back.

"People read about a snatching," Gloria goes on, "and they say to themselves, Gee, a parent must really love a child to go to all that trouble."

But parental abductions seldom have anything to do with love. Surveys by the Stolen Child Information

Exchange show that 90% of parents who take their own children illegally are emotionally unstable or abusive. Over half have criminal records! Children most often are snatched for revenge, because the parent is angry at the court or jealous of the parent with custody.

Very often an estranged parent sends signals. Be on the lookout for:

* a change of job, possibly a move to another city
* "burning bridges," breaking of relationships
* repeated deviations from the rules of the custody agreement
* increased hostility of former in-laws or mutual friends
* overt threats of taking the child.

The majority of parental abductions occur befor custody has been determined. This is a difficult situation, but there are steps you can take to prevent it. We will discuss them in Chapter VII.

THE CHILD SNATCHERS

As with adult rape, the motive for taking children is usually an irrational drive for violence, expressed in a sexual way. Most child abductors are white, adult males. But again, there are no absolutes. In some cases there is no sexual motivation or desire to harm the child.

Kidnappings by women, usually of infants, are becoming more and more common. In a San Diego hospital, eight days after her birth in 1983, Amelia Leal

Ramirez was taken by a woman posing as a nurse. Women have also stolen children from nursery schools, shopping centers, and homes where they were baby-sitting.

A woman who takes a child often does so simply because she wants a child of her own. Or she may be acting with a male accomplice to secure children for one of the profitable baby-for-sale rings.

We mentioned earlier that most people who abduct children have no outward signs to distinguish them from other people. If you look carefully, however, below surface appearances, you can sometimes detect persons who would be more likely than others to commit crimes against children.

THE PEDOPHILES: FIXATED AND REGRESSED

"Pedophile" is a term given to an adult whose conscious sexual interests and behavior are directed either partially or exclusively toward children. Pedophiles fall into two categories. The "fixated" pedophile, usually a white male, has an attraction to young boys. Frequently he has a deep feeling of affection for his victim, and since most child molesters were themselves abused as children, a strong sense of identification with him. According to A. Nicholas Groth, director of the sex-offender program at the Connecticut Correctional Institution, the pedophile is "reenacting his own victimization, but he wants to change it into a warm and loving experience where he is in control, to purge the original fear."

It is the "fixated pedophile" who is largely responsible for the increasingly widespread problem of child pornography. His fascination with "kiddie porn" stems from many factors. Many pedophiles take pictures of their victims in lewd or suggestive poses, often to prove their talents to other pedophiles, much as the "Don Juan" boasts of his conquests. Pictures can also be used to lure children and lower their inhibitions. By showing the child photographs of children and adults in sexual encounters, the pedophile tries to convince him that this is acceptable behavior. He often takes photographs of his own sexual encounter with the child, so that he may have the thrill of reliving the experience. Child molesters often have thousands of photographs of their victims in elaborate filing systems.

The state of Kentucky, with its Task Force on Exploited and Missing Children, has led the way in identifying the pedophile. In an all-out investigation, they uncovered some startling cases of child exploitation and abuse:

> At a Christian Bible camp near rural Kenton County, police arrested the 28-year-old director, who allegedly had been engaging in sexual relations with minors on the camp grounds for the past three years. Owners of the financially strapped camp admitted that they had been lax in investigating backgrounds of their staff.

> In Louisville, a 52-year-old mainte-nance man was luring residents from a nearby home for needy and neglected boys with promises of custodial jobs in the nightclub where he worked. Some of the boys knew that sex with their employer would be part of the job; others found out later. About fifteen boys were

said to have been involved in an ongoing sex ring.

Also in Louisville, a wealthy businessman had been sharing his exclusive lifestyle with deprived young blacks. On Sunday, the man sat in his car outside black churches, waiting for children. One officer said he apparently "would give presents to kids who would introduce him to other kids." The man bought the children fine sport coats, drove them to fashionable restaurants in his Lincoln Continental, and entertained them at his exclusive condominium. What the children did in exchange was to pose naked for his camera. A search of his apartment uncovered hundreds of photos of naked children, all of them black.

These cases — and hundreds more — have come to light in Kentucky because concerned citizens probed and sought them out. As *Newsweek* magazine puts it, "The idea that adults might be sexually attracted to children is so offensive that most parents prefer not to think about it." They should. What's happening in Kentucky is happening in every state in the country! Irving Prager, a California attorney who used to prosecute child molesters, believes that sexual child abuse "is probably the most common serious crime against a person in the United States."

Unlike the fixated pedophile, the "regressed" offender generally is an otherwise normal heterosexual male who turns to young girls at a crisis point, such as a divorce or setback in business. Often incestual, he has been described as the "child molester who stays at home." His pedophilia is an abrupt departure from his normal sexual activity; he turns to children at the time of the stressful situation because he is genuinely aroused by them. Except for his sexual orientation toward children, the "regressed" pedophile is generally considered respectable in every way.

The victimized child is confused and frightened. He is frequently threatened by the pedophile to prevent him from telling his parents of the experience, which could involve anything from fondling to intercourse.

There is no fool-proof formula for telling a pedophile from an adult who has a genuine, healthy love for children, but there are signs you can watch for. They do not always indicate that the person is a pedophile, nor does their absence prove that he is not. However, some pedophiles do send out warning signals.

A pedophile often feels socially and sexually insecure with adults, but is much more at ease with children. He tends to be childlike himself and to treat children as equals or buddies. He may attempt to "buy" the child with such things as money or toys, or to grant privileges that are forbidden by the child's parents and certainly not in his best interests. Be very cautious of anyone who undermines the authority of parents or asks the child to lie to them or keep secrets from them.

He is often obsessed with sex, especially lewd or "kinky" sex. He enjoys looking at erotic pictures and reading "adult" books and may have many of both in his collection. His conversation, especially with children, may include suggestive remarks and a preoccupation with sex. One pedophile who worked as a school custodian liked to cut clippings out of newspapers and magazines, underline suggestive passages, and leave them on children's desks in the classroom.

He may "hang around" places where children congregate, such as parks, playgrounds or schoolyards, when he has no real reason for being there.

The regressed pedophile can be especially difficult to detect, as he often has no history of sexual preference for children.

He may surprise himself when he finds he is attracted to them. Remember that this type of pedophilia is brought about by sudden stressful situations, an abrupt departure from the usual lifestyle. The regressed pedophile is not acting at this point as he has been known to act in the past. He may send out the same warning signals as the fixated pedophile, with the signals ignored by friends and relatives who excuse him for not "being himself."

Your child may also give you clues. Never take it lightly if he reports any incidents. Children seldom lie about molestation. If he feels uncomfortable about going to day camp or nursery school, or of staying with a particular babysitter, there might be a reason. Encourage your child to tell you if he suspects any adult of having improper motives.

A big danger with both types is that they are frequently authority figures — teachers, pastors, Scoutmasters, choir leaders, etc. — and command respect in their communities. This creates a confusing situation.

Here you have a difficult task. How can you teach your child to be on the lookout for problems with people he knows—and very often trusts? Once again, communication is vital. Most friends, relatives, and acquaintances have no intention of doing him harm. He must learn which of them can be trusted. Close, trusting relationships are a very necessary part of normal growing up.

The answer is in what you, the parent, do. **Be alert to**

any potential problems, even among your own family or friends. Many abductions have occurred because a parent simply did not want to believe that this person he knew and perhaps loved would be capable of such a thing.

Be watchful of any unusually strong bond that seems to develop between your child and an adult. And never let your child spend the night alone with any adult whom you are not **very** sure of. If you feel reasonably certain a potential problem exists, let the person concerned know about it, without accusing him. Sometimes just the suggestion that you are watching will prevent problems from happening. And never leave your child alone with anyone you have any reason to suspect.

Find out about security background checks in hiring procedures of teachers, camp couselors, playground workers, custodial help — anyone who is with your children and responsible for them. If you feel the school system or other agency is lax in this, insist that they tighten up and hire no one who has not been thoroughly investigated. (See Chapter XI.)

Know your child's friends. Don't think it is old-fashioned to want to meet them and their parents. Don't let your child visit, especially overnight, with anyone you feel uncomfortable about.

Your child should learn to respect his body and his own right to privacy. He should feel comfortable about coming to you to report if anyone — including friends or relatives — should attempt to violate that right by touching him in an improper manner. Tell him that he need not submit to physical contact — hugs, kisses, etc., — if he does not want to. **Never belittle any fear or concern your child should express to you.**

We teach our children to be respectful of adults and to respect their wishes. Even if this is not emphasized as much today as it once was, children seem naturally in awe of "big people," their parents, teachers, recreation workers and adults generally, and expect all of them to act as protectors concerned for their welfare, health and safety. So what then do you tell your child? To instill a fear of all adults could do irreparable damage to a youngster with a real need to love and trust. It could also prevent him from asking for help if he should need it.

You will need a lot of **frank, open discussion**. Your child must know that he is loved, that it is your concern for his safety and well-being that is behind all this. You will want to get across to him — very vividly — that there are many more friendly and well-intentioned people in the world than there are those who would wish to do him harm. Unfortunately, however, the "bad guys" don't always wear black hats or trench coats. We just have no way of knowing who they are.

So all the old warnings your parents gave you apply more than ever today:

> *   Never talk to strangers, take rides from them, or accept gifts from them.
> *   Be cautious of anyone, especially adult men, who seem overly friendly.
> *   Be aware of the dangers of public restrooms, and know that it is safer to go anywhere with a friend than it is to go alone.

Some rules have come about more recently. Those clever T-shirts — with "Todd" or "Susan" printed in two-inch letters on the back — are a perfect way for a kidnapper to get your child's attention and trust.

Never put your child's name on his clothing, bicycle

or the outside of his school books. Teach him that a stranger is still a stranger, even one who might call him by name.

He should know what to do if someone does attempt to abduct him. **Teach him the Break Away/Get Away Techniques shown in Chapter IV.** And tell him to scream, preferably something understandable, such as, "This is not my father," as many times as necessary in order to get aid from a passerby.

All of these precautions seem so obvious that we often overlook the fact that children just won't know them unless they are told. Be sure to tell your children — not once, but many times.

CHAPTER III

THE OUNCE OF PREVENTION

How sad that men would base an entire
civilization on the legal and presumed
responsibility for children, and then
never really get to know their sons
and daughters very well.
Phyllis Chesler

BEING PREPARED

A child's world as he has experienced it is as small as he is. For this reason, he can lose his bearings more easily than an adult would. Sometimes, when the mysteries of a larger world beckon, or when a playmate suggests a new place to explore, the world gets larger than his conception of it. He becomes lost.

It is so easy for a child to lose his way.

* Directions can be confusing. East and west, left and right, mean little to a pre-schooler.
* An interesting sight or intriguing sound can beckon a small child to follow, causing him to wander out of sight.
* A new neighborhood with different landmarks takes time to become familiar. A child might try to go too far away too soon.
* Worst of all is abduction; a stranger, or more often someone known to the child, entices or forcefully takes him from familiar surroundings.

Obviously the most effective thing a parent can do is to prevent him from becoming lost in the first place. It is vital that today's parent educate his child to avoid situations that lead to tragedy.

Not all child abductions are preventable. Johnny Gosch of West Des Moines, Iowa, came from a close

41

family where the children were well supervised. His mother, a firm believer in the "buddy system," insisted that he never leave alone for his early morning paper route. On the morning he was abducted, he was accompanied by four other boys. One of the boys reported later that Johnny commented on a man following him whom he described as "weird." Soon afterwards, Johnny was seen being forced into an automobile by two men. He hasn't been seen since.

"All the prevention measures available sometimes don't help," his mother says. "We did everything we could — and still our son is gone."

But many others could have been prevented—had parents been aware of the dangers.

Children wander away from shopping centers, from theatres, from parks, beaches and other recreational areas. Kidnappings have occurred on the way home from school, church and Scout meetings. A tremendous number of children disappear from their own homes or yards. No place is truly immune from danger.

As a parent you need to know what safety measures to take in all of these places. You need to be totally prepared at all times. And the first step is to learn all about your child — his habits, his routines, his sports, hobbies and methods of play. Find out the most likely places to look, **before** tragedy strikes.

YOUR CHILD'S TERRITORY

Children feel comfortable with familiar patterns. For this reason, most of the time their lives develop and settle into fairly regular routines. If you carefully examine the leisure-time activities of your child, you will most likely see a familiar consistency. Certain areas of play are favorites; usually one or two friends are preferred over the others. As tactfully as possible, without appearing to invade his private world, you need to find out these patterns. Who are his friends? Where do they live? Where do they usually go to play — to parks and playgrounds? Or do they prefer to go behind a hedge, under a bridge, or in an old shed?

Most adults can remember the need of a child to "belong" to an exclusive group of his peers, the joy of shared secrets, the fun of a secret hideout. For children, privacy is important. But it is vital that you know your child's whereabouts at all times. Let him know that you respect his privacy, but that you need to know where he is and who he is with when he is away from you. Take the time to make it clear that it is because of your love and concern for him that you must know these things.

When you taught your child to cross the street, you made him aware of the dangers, but also let him know that there was a correct and safe way for him to do it. This is what you must do in describing the very real dangers of kidnapping and abduction. The dangers exist, but in most cases can be prevented with common sense and planning. The more knowledge and preparation the child has, the less he has to fear.

Cover your child's territory with him. Walk with him to school. Look for distractions or potential hazardous areas along the way. If he does not follow a regular planned route, make one with him. Tell him places where he can go — to a store, gas station, office, or home of someone you know — if he should encounter suspicious strangers or dangerous situations. Ask him to show you those "secret" places, and assure him that you'll keep it secret. Take a walk with him around the park or playground where he goes to play.

SURROUNDING TERRITORY

Sooner or later your child will want to branch out, to explore places close by but away from the usual territory. In this new and larger world, without familiar landmarks, it can be very easy for him to lose his bearings, to become confused and lost.

Take another walk with him. Show him how the world beyond the one he knows opens up and connects with familiar pathways, how he can find his way back should he find himself on unfamiliar turf.

Teach him to memorize new landmarks — buildings, trees, shrubs, signs, or unusual houses. Point these out, making sure that they are unlikely to be changed, uprooted, or torn down. Show him how the streets are marked; teach him the name and number patterns of streets and avenues — indicating which run north and south and which run east and west. Point out names of streets that are close to each other or that will lead to home or school.

Vacant lots, empty buildings, new construction sites and excavations are **not** safe places to play. Make this clear to him. Explain why. Again, show him where to go if he does get confused or lost.

Who are the "friendly" adults in this area — policemen, security guards, recreation workers, store clerks — who will help a child if he needs it? You may first need to find out yourself. Be sure, before you introduce them to your child, that they are responsible and trustworthy.

Some friendly visits to stores, service stations and offices in the area can help the child, especially if he is very young or very shy, to feel more at home with these people. He can talk with them, or purchase an item, so that he will see them as friends. Later on, you can include their names in casual conversation and refer to them in family discussions. He will soon learn to trust them and to know that they can be relied upon should he ever need their help.

MAPS

Maps are invaluable in familiarizing the child with his territory and the places that surround it.

Buy a map of your city, and if your child is old enough, teach him how to read it. For younger children, draw a simple map of your own neighborhood and surrounding area, or let him make his own. Find the locations of your home, the school, church, shopping malls or other places you visit frequently. Let your child find where his friends live. Review with him the safest route home from these places.

Take your maps along and follow them when you go on your "explorations." Together, find important landmarks: the school, neighborhood park or playground and other well known places. Trace the route you took on the map. Identify the names of streets you walked. Discuss the things you saw along the way. The more you do this, the more your child will identify with his territory and feel at home in it, thus lessening his chances of becoming overwhelmed and engulfed by it.

KNOWING YOUR CHILD

Too often problems occur because the parent doesn't really know his child — starting with what he is wearing that day and including such factors as his basic personality, the way he feels about things and people, his basic fears — in short, the child as a person. (It isn't uncommon for children to tolerate sexual abuse for years, simply because they don't know how to tell someone about it.)

Be sensitive to any changes in behavior or attitudes. Encourage open communication. Make it a point to really get acquainted, for more reasons than just security. Children who feel free and open with their parents, who can talk to them about their fears, concerns, and innermost feelings, are much less likely to run away or to be in a position to be taken away.

One of the most important things you can do for your child is to let him know that you will listen, not just advise and admonish, when he talks to you. In this way you'll discover trouble spots before they become real problems.

THE TELEPHONE

Never underestimate the power of the telephone! More than any other instrument, it has played a vital part in the return of thousands of lost children. Stress its importance to your child. Teach him as much about using it as he is capable of understanding. You might point out how E.T. learned to call home and that he can do the same.

A three-or four-year-old can learn to dial the "0" for Operator. A four- or five-year-old can learn his own telephone number, along with the area code. If the child is old enough, teach him how to dial his number, how to dial long distance direct, and how to call collect. Help him memorize the emergency number in your area. This information could save his life.

The many styles of telephones, with different types of dials, can be confusing, so let him practice on all types, including pay phones. He can call grandparents or friends from a store, restaurant or the movies. **When he leaves home, be sure he has his phone number written down** in case he forgets it or becomes confused during stress. Tape the number in an inconspicuous place on his bicycle, or on an object that he usually carries with him; write it in indelible pen on a label inside his jeans or inside a shoe or belt. Be sure he always has enough money with him to use a pay phone if he should need to. Show him how to use the public charge phones that require no money and will charge the call to his home phone.

Most phones, public and private, display the number, including the area code. Your child should know where to look for this number. Even if he can't tell you where he is when he calls, police can find his location from the telephone number. If you receive a call from your child that he is lost, get this number immediately. If he cannot give it to you, keep him on the telephone and call the police from another phone. In an emergency situation they will have the call traced, but they can only do it while the caller remains on the phone.

Check to see if your community has the "enhanced" 911 system. With this system the child can dial 911 (pay phones require no money for this) and even if he leaves the phone, the police will know the location and will dispatch a patrol. It is important, however, that the phone remain off the hook. Tell the child not to hang up, even if for any reason he cannot speak or must leave the phone.

HOME SAFE — OR IS IT?

In 417 cases of child disappearance reported by the Dee Scofield Center, a Florida organization that is researching the problem of child abductions, over one - third of children reported missing were taken from their own home or yard.

Your home may not be as safe as you think. Especially for pre-schoolers, your front yard might be the most dangerous part of it. Not only is it very easy to wander away from, but it is usually accessible to anyone — stranger or not — who may want to abduct your child.

Your back yard may be more private, but even if it is completely fenced in, **don't** leave your child alone or unattended there. The ways an inquisitive child can devise for discovering what is on the other side of the fence would astound you.

Even in the best of circumstances, in the most respectable of neighborhoods, it is never safe to leave a pre-schooler at home alone. If you must leave an older child (between six and ten) alone, make your absence very brief, no longer than twenty or thirty minutes, depending on the maturity and responsibility of the child. Let a neighbor know you will be gone for a few minutes.

Remind the child of the emergency number and how to use it, or tell him he can dial the operator to report an emergency. Tell the child and the neighbor where you are going and when you will be back. **Leave a phone number** with both of them where you can be reached.

Lock all doors, and instruct your child not to open them to anyone he doesn't know. Tell him that if a stranger does become aware he is home, to act as if you are home in the shower or unable to come to the door.

Children returning home alone from school or play can walk into potentially dangerous situations — a robbery in progress, for example. Teach your child to make a quick check before entering the house. An open door or window or an unfamiliar vehicle in the driveway can be warning signals.

If your child should become missing, one of the first things you will be asked is what he was wearing. Even if he is just playing in the back yard, be sure each day to make a mental note, or a written one if necessary, of everything he is wearing — including coats, hats, jewelry, scarves, mittens, boots or shoes.

SCHOOL

Where would a child abductor go to look for a victim? Logical places would be schools, playgrounds, public parks — anywhere large groups of children congregate. He undoubtedly knows the routes they take to and from these places, when they are unsupervised and most vulnerable. About 30% of abducted children are taken from schoolgrounds or parks, or when they are enroute to or coming home from these places. Most of these abductions occur in broad daylight and within sight of other people.

Just how much protection your child will need walking to and from school or his bus stop depends on many factors — the age of the child, the type of neighborhood he has to walk through, the amount of traffic he will encounter, the length of his journey. If you feel it is necessary, walk or drive him yourself and **be sure he is safely on board his bus or in his classroom** before you leave. Better to be accused of being an overprotective parent than to have your child join the list of statistics.

It is always safer for children to **travel in pairs** or groups than alone, and it's even better if an adult or older child can go along. If at all possible, make sure your child does not have to walk to school or to his bus stop alone. Stress to him the importance of coming directly home after school, unless you have made other arrangements with him.

A talk with teachers, counselors, and administrators should indicate to you just how they feel about the responsibility for the safety of your child while he is at school. They are responsible, whether or not they acknowledge the fact, for such things as seeing that your child is supervised at all times, letting you know in advance if he has to stay after hours and barring people from the school grounds that have no business being there.

The school should also call you if your child is absent. If it does not do this as a regular policy, take action, with other parents if necessary, to see that it does. (See Chapter XI.) Be sure to call if you know your child will be absent for any reason.

SHOPPING

Shopping with a rambunctious youngster in tow can be a trial for the most patient of mothers. In shopping malls, supermarkets and department stores, attractions for children abound. With crowds of people a child can easily slip away and get lost, making him easy prey for abduction.

Check out the shopping area before you take your youngsters there. Make sure the stores you will be visiting have a safe environment. The store personnel—owners, managers, security people and sales clerks—should be concerned for the safety of children, with an insistence on proper "store manners" along with a concern for their welfare.

Plan your trip in advance. Tell your children where you will be going and what you will be doing. Instruct them in how to behave while you are there, making it clear that they must not become separated from you. Most malls have a diagram or map of the mall in a central court. When you get to the mall, show your child the diagram, pointing out where you are then and where you are going. If there is an information or security booth, show it to him on the diagram and take him to it so that he can find it if he needs to.

You will frequently hear parents admonishing their children by name, in a supermarket, for example. This is also an opportunity for a potential snatcher to learn your child's name, which he can then use to lure him outside, into a storeroom, or elsewhere out of your control. If it is necessary to use the child's name to correct him or get him under control, hold him close to you and speak so he alone can hear.

Another suggestion: Each time you go to the shopping mall, the fairgrounds, the city park or other places where there may be crowds and where the child could become separated from you, **use a code name or word**. Talk about it with the child and decide on one for use that day. Choose one that is easy to remember, such as the name of a pet. Tell him that if for any reason you and he should become separated, he is to go with no one unless the code name or word is used in a message from you. He will have fun playing Agent 007, and you will feel a little more secure about taking him to crowded places.

Never leave a child under ten anywhere by himself. If you absolutely **must** leave an older child alone for a few minutes, discuss it with him beforehand. Tell him where you are going to be, where you expect him to be, and how soon you will be back. Review the plan on the way, and do not vary from it.

If you must leave a child under ten alone in a car, be sure that it is for no more than a few minutes. Make certain the car doors are locked and windows are secured, but open enough to give him air. Teach him to honk the horn continuously if a stranger tries to open the door and to stay in the car until you return. Explain to him where you will be, why you cannot take him along, and when you will return. Set a definite time limit, ten minutes or less, and be there when you say you will. If a policeman or guard is patrolling the area, ask him to keep an eye on your child.

Harnesses used to be common for use with small children in public places. They are still available and today, more than ever, a good idea. Pre-schoolers should never leave your sight. Some require constant, close attention, and you simply do not have enough hands to shop and hold onto an active child at the same time.

Those wallet-sized pictures of your children can have much more than sentimental value. **Keep a photo of each of your children in your purse or wallet**, just in case you should get separated, and check to be certain they are there before you leave the house.

WHICH CHILDREN ARE VULNERABLE?

Some children are more vulnerable than others. These are usually the quiet, thoughtful ones, those who seem to have special and intense needs for adult affection and approval. They may be the children you would call loners, the ones who are withdrawn, unable to relate socially to children of their own age — those who seem to be unable to have fun spontaneously, who are lacking in self esteem. Or they may be the ones who are chronic discipline problems, showing an unusual bravado to conceal their basic insecurity.

Many victims of child exploitation are runaways

fleeing parental abuse. Others suffer from a lack of parental attention and love, and many see their exploiter as the one who will provide it. Molesters often take children to movies, ballgames, or even on vacations, in return for sexual favors. For some lonely children, the prize of adult affection seems worth their own victimization.

But even if you feel that your child is mentally and emotionally stable, never assume that he is safe. An otherwise open, fun-loving, spontaneous child may become vulnerable in threatening life situations—a pending divorce or separation, a parent's unemployment or ill health, problems with discipline at home or in school, failure in school or in interpersonal relations with children his own age.

All children are more vulnerable in some physical situations than others; case histories have identified the following:

* Walking alone to or from school, especially after normal school hours
* Waiting for a school or city bus alone
* Waiting in an open, parked car
* Using enclosed, poorly lit stairways, corridors, and public rooms such as apartment laundries and restrooms of large public buildings, especially after normal hours
* Playing in a public park or playground after hours or after dark, or playing there unsupervised at any time
* Exploring remote areas in buildings or on the grounds of large public facilities

* Waiting in public parking lots, including those in shopping centers, after dark or normal working hours
* Riding a bicycle alone or at night
* Using late night or all night facilities, such as launderettes.

Be aware of the dangers in these situations. And be alert to any changes in your child's personality or in his home or family situation that would make him more susceptible to abduction or running away.

CHILD-PAC DATACARDS™ AND PARENTS ACTION PLAN™

The time to gather the information on your child is **before** he is ever missing. Julie Patz, mother of missing Etan, explains, "I can't tell you how difficult it is to remember all the little details — once the child isn't there. You wonder — exactly where was that mole? — even though you've looked at it every day of his life. In those first months, when there's so much emotional trauma, you start realizing how faulty memory is."

The **Child-Pac Datacards**, designed by the National Association for Missing Children after hours of consultation with police and with parents of missing children, are an essential part of the program described in this book. You will need to devote some time — a few hours, perhaps an afternoon — gathering information and writing it down. Or you may need to write or call for some of it.

Do it NOW. You'll be in no state of mind to do it when and if you should need it. If a search for your child should need to be made, it can be underway much faster if **all** this information is readily available. The investment of time you make now could be the most important one you will ever make. Be sure your information is accurate, and attach a current, clear photo of your child. A passport-sized school photo is excellent.

Update the cards at least annually, or whenever there is a change in any item. If your child should get new glasses, a drastically different hairstyle, or anything that would change his appearance, replace the photo.

Begin NOW to fill out your Parents Action Plan.

REVIEW

*   Have you explored your child's territory with him and asked him to show you his favorite places to play?

*   Have you explored the surrounding territory with him?

*   Does your child know which adults he can turn to if he should need help? Do you discuss these people often?

*   Have you pointed out landmarks your child could use to find his way home?

*   Have you made a map of your neighborhood and gone over it with your child?

*   Have you often discussed with your child the possibility of abduction, by both strangers and by people he knows, making it clear to him that **most** people have no intention of doing him harm?

*   Does he know that it is safer to travel in groups or with a friend than alone?

*   Have you checked out the backgrounds of people your child sees frequently? Have you learned the hiring procedures of his school, camp or playground?

* Have you met your child's friends and talked to their parents?

* Do you really know your child? Have you talked to him freely and openly about his feelings and the things that bother him? Does he know that you are willing to listen to his problems?

* Have you stressed the importance of the telephone? Have you taught your child as much about how to use it as he is capable of understanding? Does he know his phone number, including the area code?

* Are you careful about supervising your child when he is playing in his own yard?

* Have you instructed your child to be alert for any signs of danger when he returns home alone?

* Have you carefully thought about the safety of the trip to school or bus stop? Have you told your child the safest route to take and what to do if he should run into any problems on the way?

* Have you talked to principals and teachers? Do you feel confident that they are responsible and concerned for the child's safety?

* Does your school call to report absences? Do you always call if you know your child will not be there?

* Have you checked out shopping areas and other public places you might take your child to see if they have a safe environment? Do you plan shopping trips in advance with your children?

* Do you have a photograph of each of your children in your wallet or purse? Do you always check to see that it is there before you take your children anywhere?

* Does he know what to do if he should be abducted?

* Have you carefully and thoroughly filled out the **Child-Pac Datacards**™ and **Parents Action Plan?**™

CHAPTER IV

BREAK AWAY/GET AWAY

*A safe world? It would be like heaven.
Not exactly like heaven but just like
God wanted it to be.*

From Your Children Should Know

Can a small child learn techniques that will help him escape from the grasp of a much larger and stronger adult? The answer is yes, if the child acts **quickly** and catches the attacker by **surprise**. The element of **quickness** can often make up for the inequality in strength. When the child keeps a cool head and acts **quickly**, these maneuvers can be effective:*

THE WINDMILL

This is a basic arm trap. If the attack is from the rear, with a grab on the shoulder, the child turns toward the abductor, placing his arm on the attacker's arm to gain stability. The child **immediately** follows with a stomp to the attacker's instep. The child then runs away.

#1.
The attacker grabs the child by the shoulder.

#2.
The child immediately turns toward the attacker, placing his hand on the attacker's arm to gain stability.

*For details on the Break Away/Get Away video instructions, see page 176.

#3.
The child delivers a
stomp to the attacker's
instep.

#4.
Then the child runs
away.

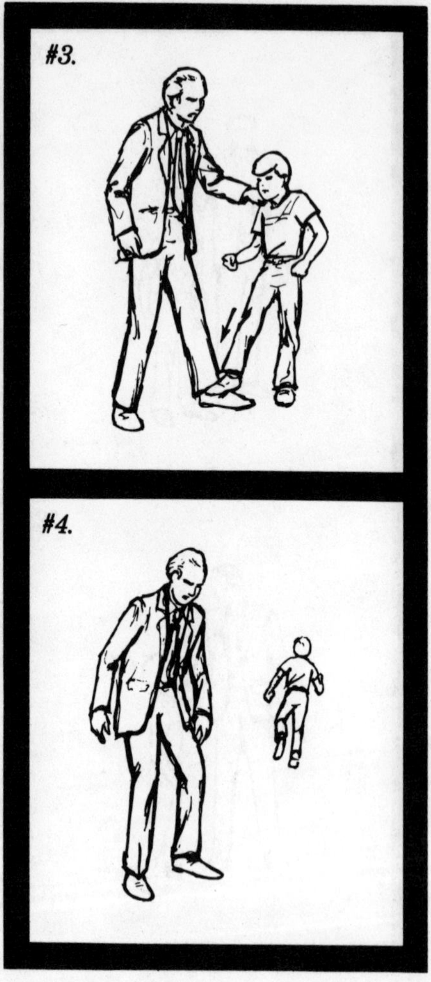

DONKEY KICKS

When the child is grabbed from the rear and lifted off the ground by the attacker, the child immediately applies heel kicks to the groin area.

#1.
The child is grabbed from the rear and lifted off the ground by the attacker.

#2.
The child immediately assumes groin kick position.

#3.
The child may apply double heel kicks, or may repeatedly keep using one foot to kick the attacker's groin area.

PULL TO THE SKY

If the abductor grabs the child's wrists, the child **immediately** turns her wrists in an upward and outward direction toward the attacker's thumbs. **Speed** is essential to break the hold.

#1.
The attacker grabs the child by the wrists.

#2.
The child immediately turns wrists in an upward and outward direction toward the attacker's thumbs.

#3.
The child breaks free.

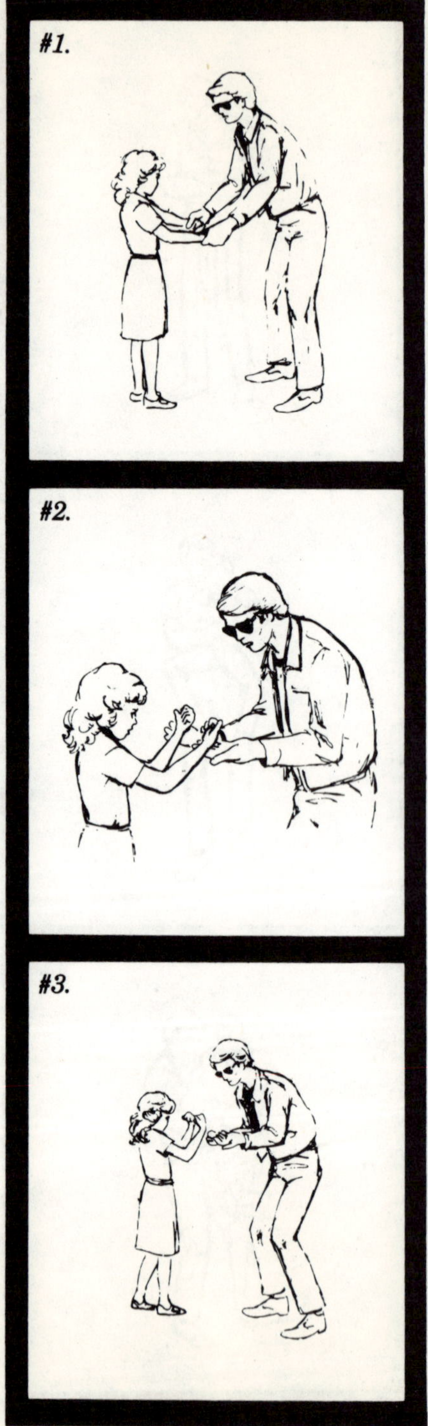

SLAP AWAY

If the abductor attempts to choke the child from the front, the child **immediately** raises both hands through the attacker's hands, and with a criss-cross motion **quickly** slaps and pushes the attacker's hands away. The pressure of the slaps and pushes forces the leverage of the hold outward.

#1.
The attacker assumes a choke position from the front.

#2.
The child immediately raises his hands through the attacker's arms.

#3.
With a criss-cross motion, the child immediately slaps and pushes the attacker's hands away.

THE RAG DOLL

If the abductor approaches from the rear and grabs both of the child's arms, the child **immediately** collapses one arm into and against his spine. This allows him to turn, so that he will have access for a stomp to the instep.

#1.
The attacker grabs both of the child's arms from the rear.

#2.
The child immediately collapses one arm into and against his spine, thereby allowing him to turn.

#3.
The child can now stomp onto the attacker's instep.

HAND ON HAND

When the child is grabbed by the hair, she **immediately** brings both hands up onto the top of the attacker's hands to alleviate the pressure of the hold. At the same time, she bends and steps back. The child stomps on the instep and pulls back, breaking free.

#1.
The child immediately places her hands on the attacker's hands to alleviate the pressure of the hold.

#2.
The child immediately steps back, kicking the attacker behind the knee.

#3.
The child continues to step back even farther. This forces the attacker's arm into an unnatural position. The child can then break free.

KEYS AND WHISTLES

The child should always carry three keys and a whistle on a keychain. One key should be placed between each of the joints of his fingers and the whistle between the thumb and index finger while the hand is held in a fist position. If approached, the child can slash the eye, ear, neck or temple areas of the abductor, freeing himself and running away while blowing the whistle.

#1.
The child should always carry three keys and a whistle on a keychain.

#2.
The attacker approaches the child.

#3.
The child should immediately attack by slashing the eye, ear, neck or temple area of the attacker, with the keys held firmly in place.

#4.
The child should immediately run away while blowing the whistle.

PUSH TO THE GROUND

To avoid a full
Nelson hold from the
rear, as the attacker's
arms are coming up
under the child's arm-
pits, the child **immedi-
ately** shoots his arms
straight down to the
ground. This stops the
leverage so the attacker
cannot get his hands up
behind the child's neck.
The child then rotates
his hips to one side and
comes back with a fist to
the groin of the attacker.

#1.
*The attacker advances
from the rear for a full
Nelson hold.*

#2.
*To avoid this hold, as the
attacker's arms are com-
ing up under the child's
armpits, the child
immediately shoots his
arms straight down to
the ground, keeping his
arms rigid.*

#3.
*The child rotates hips to
one side and comes back
with a fist to the groin of
the attacker.*

THE ROCKET

If the abductor attacks the child from the front and grabs him by the hair, the child **immediately** cups the attacker's hands to alleviate pressure and delivers a straight kick to the groin.

#1.
The attacker grabs the child from the front by the hair.

#2.
The child places his hands on the attacker's hands to alleviate the pressure of the hold.

#3.
The child immediately delivers a straight kick to the groin.

CHAPTER V

MISSING — THE FIRST HOURS

*Childhood is frequently a solemn business
for those inside it.*

George T. Will

SYSTEMATIC SEARCH

The first hour of the search is the most crucial.

Thousands sympathized with John Walsh in the 1983 television reenactment of the abduction of his six-year-old son Adam. In a frantic but futile effort to enlist the help of the F.B.I. on the first day Adam was missing, Walsh, in total frustration, declared, "The F.B.I. will go after stolen trucks and missing race horses, but won't do as much for a lost child." In 1981, when Adam was kidnapped, F.B.I. policy was to wait 24 hours after the disappearance, unless there was a ransom demand or clear sign of a kidnapping.

Thanks to the efforts of Walsh and others, such as Florida Senator Paula Hawkins, who introduced the Missing Children's Act in the Senate and saw it signed into law in 1982, this is no longer the case. The law allows parents to contact the F.B.I. directly. It also made the F.B.I.'s National Crime Information Center's (NCIC) computer available to store information on cases of missing children. When four-year-old David Edward Rattray was abducted from his home in Vero Beach, Florida, in early 1983, dozens of F.B.I. agents immediately converged on the case — without waiting for a ransom demand. The child was found locked in the trunk of a car and was returned home in a few days.

Etan Patz was not so lucky.

On May 25, 1979, at 7:30 a.m., six-year-old Etan left his Manhattan home under the watchful eye of his mother for his school bus stop. It was the first time he had walked alone, so Julie Patz carefully reviewed the safety rules with her son and watched until he rounded the corner for the bus stop, a half block away.

It was not until that afternoon that Julie had any cause for alarm. Etan usually returned home about 3:15.

Patrolman Richard Weick posts the picture of a missing girl on a board in San Francisco's Park police station on the fringe of the Haight-Ashbury district, one-time hippie mecca. San Francisco police believe at least 20,000 runaway youths are drawn each year to the area which they say has slipped from the netherworld to the underworld.

But at 3:40 he still had not arrived. When she called the school, she learned that he had never been there that day.

In four years, the only clue to Etan's disappearance is an unverified report that he was seen getting into a car about 7:45 the morning he vanished. Intensified police action and scores of searches with bloodhounds, helicopters and psychics have produced no other valid leads.

The tragic cases of Adam Walsh, Etan Patz and thousands of other lost children have brought home an obvious fact: **The sooner the search begins, the better the chance of finding the child.**

If you discover your child missing, the most important thing is to stay calm. Easy to say, but hard to do? Not if you remember that at this stage the odds are overwhelmingly in your favor. The great majority of lost children are found, most within a few hours.

For years, overburdened police forces discouraged parents from calling them until they had reason to believe the child was in danger. But many parents of missing children have said that the one thing they would have done differently would have been to call the police sooner. Don't feel guilty about calling them immediately, if you feel it is necessary. In most states the law requires police to take a report and provide assistance.

Using the **Child-Pac Datacards,** give the police all the information on the child. Tell them what action you have taken, whom you have called, and what you have learned.

The police will put the child's description on an APB (all points bulletin) so that cruising patrol cars can watch for him. If they are hesitant about this, insist. Ask that it be done while you are on the phone.

An officer will come to your house to interview you. This is the most important part of the investigation. He will want the full description you have on the **Child-Pac Datacards** and the most recent photograph. He will probably ask you questions about your child's habits and activities. He will also most likely ask you about any problems in the family.

Here is where your **complete honesty is crucial.** One woman delayed the recovery of her child for hours because she failed to report the most likely suspect, a former lover. She was afraid the police would give the information to her husband.

You can be assured that, due to the nature of their job, law enforcement officers are virtually shockproof and will not reveal confidential information to anyone. **Don't let your own pride interfere with your child's safety.** Give the police complete information about family or marital problems if they ask for it.

Insist that your child's name, date of birth and physical description be called into the National Crime Information Center (NCIC) computer in Washington, D.C. The information will go out to precincts across the country. Confirm this by calling your local office of the F.B.I.

Once law enforcement agencies have been brought into the case, **don't leave your phone unattended.**

Take out the **Parents Action Plan** and use it. Look first in the likely spots — the back yard, the neighbor's yard, behind bushes. Check out all of the places your child frequents. Call the school. He may have had to stay after hours, or he might have missed the bus.

If he attends different classes, check attendance in each class. This can help pinpoint the time of disappearance. Using the **Parents Action Plan**, call your child's friends, starting with his best friend.

If he came to school and left on the bus, call the bus driver (listed on the **Parents Action Plan**) to find out if he got off with another child, or if the driver noticed anything unusual at the bus stop. If he didn't arrive at school, ask for names of other children who ride the same bus. Call their homes for information.

Teachers and other adults who work with your children can be valuable sources of information. Not only can they tell you about your child's whereabouts that day, but they might recall past actions or incidents that would have a bearing on the disappearance. Get their numbers from the **Parents Action Plan** and call them.

Continue to call his friends. They may be trying to protect him if the disappearance was intended to punish or evade you. Explain to them the seriousness of the situation and your real concern. Also, his friends might know of some reason for the disappearance that you would never suspect.

Call grandparents and other close relatives. **If you are separated or divorced, call the other parent.** He could be a key source of information. **Keep a list of people with whom you have spoken. Keep notes and be specific.** Write down the date and time of each call and who said what.

If these calls fail to turn up any information, organize a group of volunteers—friends, neighbors, people in the community you know you can trust — to help you with the calling. This will free your phone for incoming calls. Ask the volunteers to call every child in your child's class and every hospital emergency room in your area, with a description of the child and the clothes he was wearing.

IN PUBLIC PLACES

Crowds of people in shopping malls, department stores, amusement parks, and athletic stadiums make it easy — and very dangerous — for a child to become separated from his parents. If you find your child missing in such a place, **notify the store, mall or park security at once.** Give them the description of your child, including what he is wearing. Ask security to announce over the public address system that your child is lost and where he should come to find you.

Security officers will systematically search the store, looking in the most likely places first, then aisle by aisle, department by department. Remind them to check the rest rooms.

Most children will be found in a few minutes. If after half an hour your child is still missing, security should **notify the police.** If they hesitate, insist. If they still hesitate, call the police yourself. Ask them to meet you at the place where you will be waiting for your child.

Give the police officers your child's description, the circumstances of his becoming lost, and the child's photo in your wallet or purse. They will then continue to search with security.

If the child is not found within a reasonable time, the police will probably suggest that you return home. **Use the same route returning that you took coming.** Tell people in gas stations, small stores, etc., along the way that your child is missing; give them his description, and ask them to call the police if they should see the child or recall anything that might have a bearing on the disappearance.

At home, use the same calling and search procedures as with a child lost at home or on the way to or from school. Be available to police or F.B.I. Stay by the phone.

CHAPTER VI

STILL MISSING

*Having someone wonder
where you are when you don't
come home at night is a very
old human need.*

Margaret Mead

You have called the police, given them the information on your child, and told them what you have learned from your telephone calls. They have told you what they will do next, over the next several hours.

THE F.B.I.

By this time, especially if the child is six or under, or if there are circumstances that warrant it, the F.B.I. may have entered the picture, either at your request or that of the local police. If you have not already done so, **check with the F.B.I. to see that your child's name and vital data are entered in the NCIC computer**.

The F.B.I. will probably send an agent to talk with you. He will need the same information you gave the police and will also want any health information, such as health problems that need immediate attention, medication used by the child, or special medical treatment. This is on your **Child-Pac Datacards**.

Most important, the F.B.I. will want to know if you have been contacted by anyone concerning the child — perhaps a helpful suggestion by a friend or relative, a report of someone's having seen the child, even any crank calls. Anything at this point may be an important lead.

After you have checked with everyone who might give you any information, and after you have looked in all the likely — and even some unlikely — spots, you and the law enforcement officials will need to organize a systematic, sweeping search of the area where the child was last seen.

THE SEARCH

One item on the **Parents Action Plan** calls for you to

write down the names of people and groups to contact for assistance. There are many organizations in the community you can call on. Your local Boy Scout organization is one. The Scouts, especially older Explorer Scouts, have been very helpful in other searches. The American Red Cross is another organization frequently called on for assistance. If you have a National Guard or other reserve group in your area, contact the commanding officer; ask about help in the search. And don't forget your church or lodge. Any group of people, family, friends or others, can work as a search group under the instruction and guidance of law enforcement professionals who have been trained for this type of procedure.

You should **brief the search group on the child's physical characteristics included on the datacards** and on his appearance that day, including what he was wearing when last seen. Include in the briefing the child's personality characteristics or play habits, anything that might aid in a quick recovery.

You might want to let the police handle most of the actual briefing, but you can help a great deal by putting together a **quick poster,** including a photo of the child. This can be given to those in the search and posted in local stores, on utility poles and in other conspicuous places. A printer in your community will probably be willing to help by running the copies on short notice.

THE MEDIA

One of the first things parents think of at this time is contacting newspapers, radio and TV stations. The media can be a vital tool in your child's recovery. But **contact newspapers and others only after discussing**

the situation with the police or F.B.I., if they are involved.

A news story on TV, radio or in the newspaper could discourage possible witnesses and drive them underground in the fear that they might become suspect. In their eagerness to follow up a lead, reporters can muddy a trail police are trying to follow. At the very least, you can be sure that cranks will call with time-consuming false leads.

Instead, **prepare a well-written short announcement,** giving the child's description and the locale from which he was reported missing, along with his picture, so that you will have it ready. But leave the decision on when to use it up to the experts — the police and F.B.I.

Now that the frenzy of getting the investigation and search underway has subsided, take time to take a complete inventory. You should be somewhat calmer now and thinking more clearly. **Search your memory** and try to think out what might have happened. Try to think like your child. Whatever you might come up with, write it down. Be very honest.

Do you know of anyone who might have taken your child? If separated or divorced, have you called your ex-spouse? Even if he isn't involved, he might be able to give you helpful information.

If you rule out abduction by a parent or someone else known to the child, look into other possibilities.

Could your child have left voluntarily? If so, there must be a reason. You need to think of what the reason could be. It may be nothing more than thoughtlessness or forgetfulness. But there could be others.

Pull together your knowledge of your child and his relationships with you and other family members. Are there conditions in the home that could cause him to run away? Would he be likely to accept an invitation from a friend or a stranger?

Continue to call your child's friends. This is an emergency situation, so don't worry about making a nuisance of yourself. Remember that these children have been in close contact with your child; they may know something they wouldn't tell you at first, or they might remember something they didn't think of before. Talk to their parents. They might have overheard conversations or observed actions that could provide information.

Leaving someone to answer the phone, go to the places where your child likes to go, using his routes. A toddler most likely will stay close to home; an eight-or ten-year-old could wander into the next several blocks; a teenager most likely will have gone much farther.

While you are out, talk to neighbors, service personnel and shopkeepers. And don't forget the mailman. Remember he covers the entire neighborhood.

Be alert to all clues.

In most cases, if you have made a thorough self inventory, if you have contacted everyone who might give you any information, and if you have diligently searched for clues, you will know by the fourth or fifth hour how your child disappeared — whether he ran away or was abducted — and if abducted, whether it was by a parent, other relative or someone else known to him, or by a stranger. You can then take the appropriate action.

The next two chapters deal with the special circumstances of parental kidnapping and running away. If you know who took your child, or if you have reason to suspect someone, read the chapter on parental kidnapping. Many of the pointers on how to deal with an ex-spouse can apply to anyone whose identity you know.

CHAPTER VII

PARENTAL KIDNAPPING

*When we attempt to enter a small
child's world, we come as foreigners
who have forgotten the landscape.*

Selma Trailberg

FORESIGHT AND PREPARATION

Remember, of the estimated 150,000 children who disappear each year, 100,000 are taken by their own parents. This is called "child snatching," and in most cases it happens **before** legal custody is determined.

If you are estranged from your spouse or contemplating divorce, **keep a close watch on your children**. Since it is not a crime for a parent to take a child before the determination of custody, this can be a difficult and tricky situation. And if you feel it might happen, the **wrong** way to avoid it is to try to beat your spouse to the punch by leaving with the child yourself. By "showing malice," the absconding parent greatly lessens his chances of being granted custody.

If it does happen, there are ways to deal with it, and we will discuss them later in this chapter. For now, we are concerned with prevention.

When a divorce is in process and custody is still up for grabs, you can get a restraining order which would prevent either parent from leaving the immediate area or concealing the child's whereabouts. You might also be able, through an attorney, to obtain a temporary custody order. If contested, however, this process can sometimes take a year or more.

If divorce proceedings have not yet been initiated, but you feel your spouse might take your child, ask your attorney for advice. If you can prove malicious intent, you might be able to make it illegal for him to do so.

You have an advantage if you are still married, but contemplating a divorce which your spouse is still unaware of. You can discuss the situation with an attorney and get his advice before your spouse is apt to do anything hasty. Plan your moves carefully. If at all possible, keep the situation amicable and avoid arousing undue anger and hostility.

If you are going to announce plans for a divorce or separation, never do so in argument or in the heat of anger. Make your announcement as calmly as possible, without placing blame. Since most child snatchings are done for revenge, accusations and threats can only harm your cause. An excellent book for women contemplating divorce is *Learning to Leave*, by Lynette Triere.

In any case, whether you are divorced, separated or merely contemplating either, or even if you have no plans for severing the marriage, but you feel your spouse might take your child against your wishes, legal advice is imperative. Contact an attorney and explain your situation.

One of the most effective preventive measures you can take is to carefully prepare your child. Again, you must be wary and tactful. You don't want to plant suspicion in his mind and, especially if the child is very young, you can hardly expect him to keep secrets from his other parent. But you can let him know that he must never go anywhere without your knowledge, even if it is with his own mother or father. Impress on him how important it is for you to know where he is at all times, and to tell you before he goes anywhere with anyone, including the other parent.

A favorite trick of an absconding parent is to convince the child that the other parent does not want him, that he no longer loves him. The child then reasons that it would be fruitless to contact the other parent and that he would risk rejection by doing so.

You say your child knows he is loved, that he would never fall for such a line of reasoning? But are you sure? How secure is he? How often do you show your love and reassure him of your concern? Does he know that you love him and want him to be with you? Don't simply take for granted that he does. Show him — and tell him often.

If you have custody and your child visits the other parent, insist on strict adherence to the visitation rules and on knowing where your child is at all times.

Get addresses, telephone numbers. Call regularly to check, and ask the child to call you, especially if he is going to a different location.

Try to recall all you know of the habits, personality and character of your ex. Since you were once married to him, you must know a great deal about him. What are his feelings toward you now? Is he resentful, jealous, vindictive? Is he capable of violence and of breaking the law? If he had your child, what would he do with him?

Also, in either a permanent or temporary order, make sure your child's school records are restricted to you (or someone you may designate) in writing. Make it clear to school authorities that records are not to be given out without notifying you.

Two other steps you can take that may put at least an impediment in the way of a parent who intends to abscond with your child: Notify the State Health Department where his birth records are kept that you are the custodial parent, or that custody is being determined and you have temporary custody. They will then put a red flag on his records so that they cannot be issued without your consent. Also, obtain a social security card and number for the child; it is something he will carry with him through life and will need in many situations. It can also be used as a locator if the child is of working age.

If you have the slightest suspicion that your spouse might ever try to take your child, begin immediately to build a "tracing trail." Don't wait until you need it. Keep a record of his social security number and driver's license number. These can sometimes be used for tracing purposes, but are almost impossible to get from anyone but the individual himself. Write down names, addresses and phone numbers of friends, relatives, employers and acquaintances. Make a list of places he usually visits, either for business or recreation.

Since many people assume it is safe for a child to go with his own parent, abducting parents most often strike when the child is in the custody of someone else — when he is visiting friends or with a baby sitter, or when he is at school or camp, a day care center, music lesson, or Scout meeting.

Alert anyone who is responsible for your child of the possible danger. Explain your custody situation and visitation rules to the principal or counselor at his school. Make it clear that no one is to take the child from school, or pick him up, without your written authorization. Talk to responsible people at any other place where he might be, such as a day care center or summer camp. Show them copies of the agreement and a photo of the other parent.

It isn't always easy to explain divorce to a youngster. And it isn't easy to explain that his mother or father is not one to be trusted. But if you suspect that your ex might take your child, it is vital that you **discuss the situation with the child**, alerting him to the danger without frightening him unnecessarily. Explain that his mother or father does not have the right to take him anywhere without consulting you first, that he must not go, even if told that he has your permission. Tell him that the courts have awarded him to you for his safety and security and that the other parent would be breaking the law if he is taken away. If the parent tries to take him anywhere when you are not present, the child should know that he is to explain the situation to an adult in charge.

IF YOUR CHILD IS MISSING

If you are divorced or separated and your child disappears, it is a fair assumption that your spouse **may** be involved in your child's disappearance. The police will certainly make this a first point to investigate. You can help.

If you suspect your ex-spouse, contact him at once. (You probably have already done so. Even if he isn't involved, he is a key person to contact for information.) Explain the legal ramifications. Parental abduction by the non-custodial parent — custodial interference —is against the law. In 44 states, it is a felony to take a child from the state without the custodial parent's permission, to conceal a child within the state contrary to a court order, or to remove or conceal one during and pending custody proceedings.

This, of course, is assuming you can locate the other parent. If you don't know where he has taken your child, you need to launch a full-scale search to find him. In most cases, **locating the absent parent is the key to finding the child.**

Jim DeGray of Tampa, Florida, is a divorced father who spent seven years looking for his daughter, Karrie-Ann. Although his was not a custody dispute — Jim never questioned that it was in Karrie-Ann's best interest to remain with her mother — he did feel he was entitled to his legal visitation rights. "I just wanted to see my little girl," he explains.

Jim became obsessed with the hope of finding his daughter. For seven years he bucked the system, finding nothing but frustration and a total lack of sympathy for his plight. Judges and law officers told him repeatedly that since he didn't have custody, there was nothing they could do. A private investigator was of little help. "I found that people were turned off when questioned by a P.I.," he said. "I had better results when I talked to them myself."

Jim's most startling find was an amazing lack of knowledge by judges and law enforcement officials as to the laws governing the rights of both custodial and non-custodial parents. By delving in libraries, poring over statute books, and talking to hundreds of people, he became an expert on laws concerning child abduction, especially parental kidnapping.

He also became committed to the cause of finding lost children. Now successfully reunited with Karrie-Ann and on friendly terms with his ex-wife, Jim supports himself by doing odd jobs and spends the rest of his time working gratis for the cause. His life consists of long days of hard work, with only bare necessities to show for it. Why does he do it? "Because I believe in it," he says. He hopes to spare other parents the frustration and heartbreak he has experienced.

But he still has painful memories of the past. And he has much advice to give to others in his situation. "Of course the first thing you do when your child is missing," he says, "is to contact the police immediately. Police sometimes shy away from this type of case and will try to tell you that it's civil, not criminal, and thus out of their hands.

"But if you have legal custody, and the other parent has either abducted the child or has not returned him on time from the visitation period, then it **is** criminal. Tell the police they **have** to make a report, the same as with any missing child."

BEFORE CUSTODY

If custody has not been determined, even if you are not yet divorced, there are still steps you can take to recover a parentally abducted child. Keep in mind, however, that in this case, it is a civil, not a criminal matter. Police cannot help you locate your spouse. Your best bet is to contact one of the organizations listed in Chapter XII for help. Then you can proceed with the search on your own.

Here again, legal advice is imperative. Because technically your spouse has deserted you, you can probably get an uncontested divorce and be awarded custody of the child. If you decide to go this route, you should take the steps while the child is still missing. Ask your attorney to draw up custody papers for you.

When you locate your spouse, if he is in the same state, you can then have him served with papers. If you find him in another state, you will have to have the custody order transferred. You will also have to file a separate petition in the new state, get a court date there, and show certified copies of the custody papers.

But as with any missing child, you have to find him first.

FINDING YOUR CHILD

Most states have a computer that hooks into the NCIC computer. Police usually check the state computer first. Be sure your child's name is in both. About a week after you have requested it, call to check to see if he is still listed.

If your child is school age, the other parent will probably want to put him in school before he is gone very long. Ask the school to let you know if another school requests his records to be transferred.

Under the terms of the **Family Education Rights and Privacy Act (FERPA)** the school **must** give any parent access to school records. You may also obtain copies of anything transferred. The school must tell you where your children's records have been sent and the name of the requesting school.

Jim DeGray terms FERPA, "the **major** law to aid parents of missing school-age children." If the school does not meet the terms of the law, it can be denied federal aid. And, as Jim puts it, "We all know that no school today can operate for more than two days without federal aid." He describes the procedure for implementing the law:

Write a letter to the school the child last attended, with a certified copy of the divorce decree. Explain that under FERPA they have 45 days to turn over any request they receive from any other school district in the country for a transfer of records. At the same time, send a copy of the letter to:

FERPA Office
U.S. Dept. of Education
Room 4050, Switzer Bldg.
Washington, D.C. 20205

Sample letters to be written to help searching parents.

Your Address
City, State, Zip Code
Date

Name of School
School Address
City, State, Zip Code

To Whom It May Concern:

Please let me know if you receive a request for the transfer of records of my (son/daughter, name of child), who attended your school from ________________ to ________________.
My child is missing, and I have reported it to the proper authorities. Under the Family Education Rights and Privacy Act, you are required by law to inform me within 45 days of any request for a transfer of records.
I am sure you are aware of the urgency of this request, and I would appreciate any help you can give me. I hope to hear from you soon.

Sincerely,

(Your Name)

cc: Family Education Rights and Privacy Office
      U.S. Dept. of Education
      Room 4050, Switzer Bldg.
      Washington, D.C. 20205

*Modified from material supplied by Missing Children. . .Help Center

Your Address
City, State, Zip Code
Date

Family Education Rights and Privacy
U.S. Dept. of Education
Room 4050, Switzer Bldg.
Washington, D.C. 20205

To Whom It May Concern:

I have enclosed a copy of a letter I sent to the (Name of School) in (Address, City, State), regarding my (son/daughter, name of child), who has been reported missing.

I understand that under Federal Law I have a right to have copies of request for transfer of school records, and other information the school might have. This information must be received within 45 days or your organization may become involved.

Thank you for your time in this matter.

Sincerely,

(Your Name)

*Modified from material supplied by Missing Children. . .Help Center

Mail these letters "Certified Return Receipt Requested" so that you will know when they have been received.

If the school refuses to cooperate, write to the FERPA office, telling them you want them to become involved. They will notify the school that it has 45 days to turn over a request for a transfer of records.

If you feel that the school has had sufficient time to comply with the law but has not done so, write or call the U.S. Department of Justice. They will send a certified letter to the school notifying them that federal funds will be discontinued. And then, you can be sure you will get some action.

Jim warns that schools often do not like to be pressured by FERPA and some will make it as difficult for you as possible. He tells of one school that waited until the 44th day to comply, "just for spite." You may need to step on a few toes and doggedly persist to get the cooperation you need.

For pre-school age children, check with your pediatrician or family doctor to see if he has had a request for a transfer of medical records.

The next step is to contact an attorney — immediately — or Legal Aid if you can't afford one. He can get a court date for you to go before a judge. Under the **Parental Kidnapping Prevention Act** (PKPA) the judge can sign a felony warrant. This authorizes the Federal Parent Locator Service to help locate the child. The law states that a state or U.S. Attorney can request that the Social Security Department trace a parent through a social security number (if you have it). With the warrant, the F.B.I. can be brought into the case if it should become necessary.

The problem with this is that many judges are **unaware** of the urgency of the problem of parental kidnapping. Like many others, they assume that a child is safe with his own parent. Also, since the laws are fairly new, some judges are not familiar with them. Jim found that the felony warrant was issued in only 36% of the cases. An urgent need exists to educate judges to the new laws and the severity of the problem. Like Jim DeGray, Margaret Strickland became an expert on the laws concerning parental kidnapping when it happened to a member of her family, in this case her grandson. Her book, *How to Deal With a Parental Kidnapping* (Rainbow Books, P.O. Box 1069, Moore Haven, FL 33471), gives the full text of many of the new laws, plus an explanation of them. Included in the book is a bonus section, *Child-Snatched*, which tells Margaret's story.

If you do not file criminal charges, you have a weaker position, but you can still **ask the police to issue a "Be on the lookout for . . ." (BOLO) bulletin** on the teletype to police departments across the country.

If there is any chance that your spouse might take the child out of the country, write the Department of State and ask that the child **not** be issued a passport. Send a certified copy of the divorce decree showing that you have custody.

In what may seem like a very short time, law enforcement officials will tell you they have done all they can.

But there is still much that you can do.

Ask yourself: Why would your ex want to take your child? Is he using the child as a weapon to force you to take — or refrain from — some type of action that concerns the two of you? **Make an inventory of possible reasons. Write them down.**

Your most effective tool of investigation is to appeal to people who can give you information — employers, fellow workers and employees of businesses patronized by your spouse.

You will soon develop a feeling as to which people

sympathize with you and which do not want to become involved. You might find some who have been in similar situations and are glad to help.

Some places you can go to find information are:

1.   YOUR EX-SPOUSE'S PLACE OF WORK

Ask if he has been transferred and if so, where? If he no longer works there, where did they send his last paycheck? Ask if any other companies have called to ask for references. Talk to fellow workers who may be able to recall something he might have said to indicate where he was going.

2.   BUSINESS CONTACTS

Check with banks, credit card companies, brokers, insurance companies and agents, magazine or mail order subscriptions. (Credit cards and bank account information should be on your **Child-Pac Datacards**.) Contact them for information on change of address. (You might have better luck if you give the impression that you are not estranged from your spouse and that you are calling to verify the change.)

3.   UTILITY COMPANIES

Again, call to **verify** change of address. Ask them to read you the new address to see if it is correct.

4.   THE POST OFFICE

He might have left a forwarding address, but if he didn't want to be found, this is unlikely.

5.   PHYSICIANS AND DENTISTS

Your ex may have asked to have records transferred. Ask the nurse or secretary to read the new address to you to verify the change.

6.   FRIENDS AND RELATIVES

List everyone who knows your ex, from casual acquaintances to his closest friend or relative. Include his new spouse, if he has one, or anyone with whom he may be romantically involved. Don't forget employees of business places he patronizes — bartenders, barbers, office workers, store clerks.

Call the people on your list. Tell them you merely want to know if your child is well and safe. Ask for their help in getting in touch with your ex or at least getting word to him. As with other contacts, be tactful and courteous. They may volunteer information or give clues without realizing it. Never threaten law suits or police involvement. You can dry up leads and drive possible informants underground.

If, however, you have good reason to believe that any of these people are involved in the abduction, and if they refuse to cooperate with you, file suit against them. This might force them to help you.

When the police or F.B.I. become involved, they will be able to get this information without difficulty. However, if you have started the inquiry on your own and can share this information with them, it will help to speed the search.

Since the search will take intense involvement and a great deal of time, you may want to hire a private investigator — but this can be costly. $2,500 is a customary first fee; a long, involved search will cost much more.

Some of the organizations listed in Chapter XII can help you find an investigator if you decide to use one. Check out anyone you intend to hire with your local office of the Better Business Bureau, or with police or F.B.I. agents who have worked with them, perhaps on similar cases.

In many cases the absent parent, to satisfy his own need for revenge, will make it known by a letter or phone call that he has the child. Ask the police to wire tap your phone, in case this should happen. The call can then be easily traced.

WHEN YOU LOCATE YOUR CHILD

Once you have located your child and have definitely determined that he is with the other parent, **file charges**, if you have not already done so, but don't leave the case totally in the hands of the court. Your ex may evade them again. This happens all too frequently.

If the abduction takes place **after** custody has been determined by the courts, there is no legal question as to which parent's rights have been violated. The law has a system of recourse established to deal with such cases.

But as Gloria and Ray Yerkovich discovered in the

long search for Gloria's daughter, Joanna, the law usually deals with parental abductions in the same way as with any other domestic dispute — hands off. Through Child Find, their newly created organization, the Yerkoviches are working to force the law to handle these cases as they would any other abduction.

CHAPTER VIII

RUNAWAYS

How can I run away, when I don't know where I am?

Natasha Lang

ADOLESCENTS IN FLIGHT

The bulk of missing children — over a million each year—are runaways. One family in seven will experience a child running away.

Reasons for running vary. One 15-year-old left because her mother refused to buy her a pair of designer jeans. Others run from what they consider unreasonable demands, from verbal abuse, beatings, sexual molestation. Others simply feel unwanted. Almost all leave home without any idea of where they will eventually go or how they will get along on their own.

A pamphlet published by the Public Affairs Committee speaks of "one of the most troubled sectors of American youth, adolescents in flight" and describes running away as "a new phenomenon on the American social landscape." The problem is not new, but the large numbers of runaways today testify to one of society's most rapidly growing problems — the breakdown of the family.

To be sure, some runaways still take off from sheer boredom or a desire to get their own way. But these are in the minority. The estimate of runaways who qualify as "spoiled brats" is only about 10 percent. Today's runaway bears little resemblance to Huckleberry Finn or the "flower children" of the 60's. He is, in most cases, a severely troubled youngster, crying for attention and love, running not **to** something but **away** from problems he feels powerless to control.

According to a survey made by the Opinion Research Corporation for the Department of Health, Education and Welfare (H.E.W.), runaways were "significantly more likely" to come from single-parent households or households where both parents worked. They had low aca-

Runaways, Sacramento, California.

demic aspirations, did poorly in school, were often truant, and felt that their teachers had a low opinion of them. Many are known as "throwaways" or "pushouts." These are youths whose families have overtly or covertly spurred their departure.

Interviews with thousands of runaways disclose a constantly recurring theme — inability to communicate with parents and feelings of helpless rage over what they perceive to be gross injustices. Often disclosed, once a sympathetic listener has been found, are evidences of serious family flaws: divorce, desertion, alcoholism, mental illness, sexual promiscuity, verbal or physical abuse. Poverty is sometimes a factor, but runaways come from homes in all economic brackets.

One 15-year-old gave as his reason for running: "My parents hassle me all the time. Everything is always my fault." Another said, "My father drinks and my mother takes pills. They're too stoned to listen when I try to talk to them." A 12-year-old girl said she was raped by her stepfather and threatened with death if she told anyone. A 16-year-old left because she was pregnant and heard that there were places where she could get an abortion without too many questions.

Edward Lewis, former director of H.E.W.'s runaway youth program, described runaway behavior as "a symptom of basic upheavals in American society." He goes on to say, "Today's children have more emotional problems than those of the 60's. The emotional load is heavier; the sensory system is exposed to more shocks than ever before. The real answer to the runaway problem lies in early intervention—shoring up the weaknesses in family structure, in education, in the total social environment."

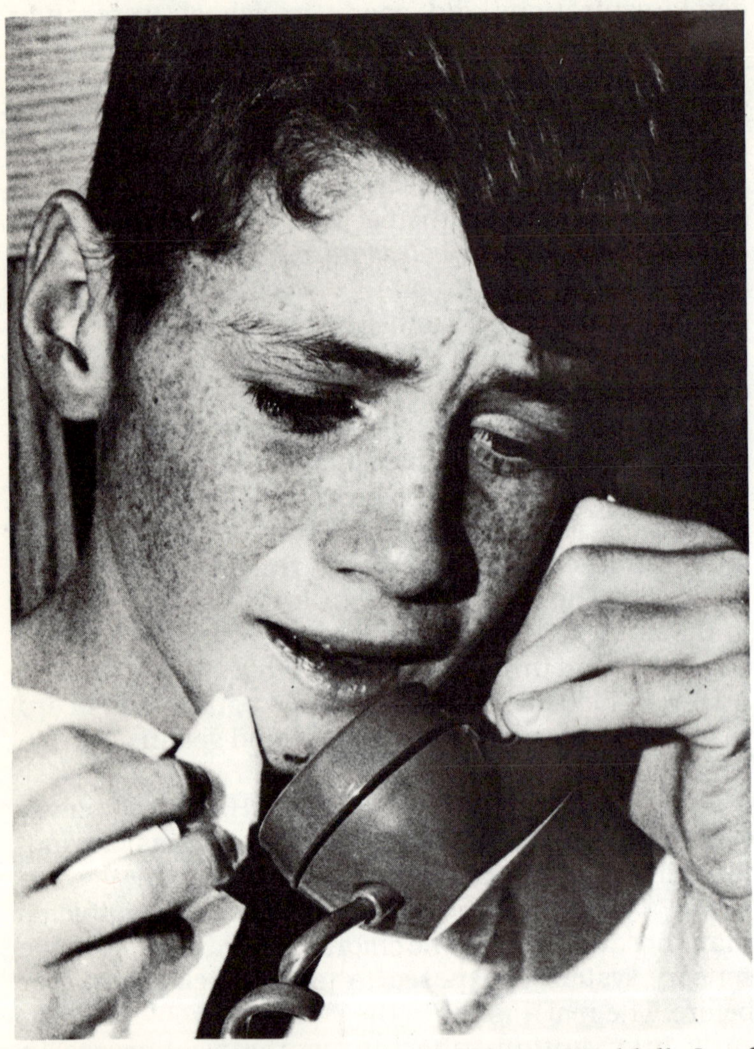

Tears spilled over as 13-year-old William Waddell, Jr., of Fayetteville, North Carolina, talks to his father on the telephone. William and a 12-year-old boy friend were found in a sealed box car where they had been locked for a 13-day, 1,000 mile journey.

SIGNALS

Even if intended for only an hour or two to punish you or get your attention, running away will take your child out of your sight and awareness of his whereabouts. It could lead to abduction by a stranger or an ex-spouse. The child could get lost or stay away longer than he intended to. Be alert to signals such as:

* Prolonged anger or resentment over disciplinary action, or withdrawal of privileges
* Fear or apprehension about conditions in the family, such as pending divorce or a new step-parent
* Problems at school, such as low grades or truancy
* Threats of running away, either overt or suggested
* Advance preparations, such as getting things together, asking directions to places he would not ordinarily go
* Requests for money, or outright theft
* Depression or withdrawal, or an unusual casualness or lightheartedness.

Most runaways come from some kind of fractured family, but the fracture is not always evident, and parents may be oblivious to these warning signals. Sanford Sherman of Jewish Family Services of New

York believes it is up to parents to "take the initiative to break down the barricades, even when they think they have done all they can and it is the child's move. Child versus parent is an unequal struggle. Parents can afford to be big about it."

WHAT YOU CAN DO

Obviously the best prevention is to have a good relationship with your child. Children seldom run when mutual respect is present, when lines of communication are open. The most frequent reason given for running is, "My parents just don't understand."

Try to understand. Listen when your children talk to you. Discuss the reasons for your rules, with possible alternatives. If you have been at fault in any situation, apologize and find a new way to work things out.

You must be firm, and you must be a parent, not just a "buddy." Your child must realize that you are the final authority. But withholding of love, or respect, or the willingness to see your child as a real person with thoughts, feelings and ideas of his own, is never effective as a disciplinary measure. It can cause resentment and hostility and create, rather than solve, problems.

Talk to your child; remember the old saying, "Teen-agers need love, too." They also need respect and parents who will listen when they talk to them. Let your teen know that you'll **be** there when he needs you.

If your child has a history of running away, or if you feel that he is showing signs of running, you need to take a close hard look at what could be the reasons. Family counseling could be the answer.

The field of psychiatry today recognizes that a troubled individual seldom becomes that way alone.

The total family structure and the interaction of the family members must be examined in order to get to the root of the problem. Some of the goals you can expect to achieve in family counseling are:

* To allow your child to express his feelings and frustrations that could trigger a runaway episode and to help him develop a relationship of trust
* To assist the child in identifying problems, seeking solutions, and developing confidence in his ability to make decisions that affect his life
* To restore communication between the child and his family and to resolve family conflicts
* To assist the child to gain a positive image of himself.

A good counselor will help the child face reality by showing him that problems can be defined and dealt with. He can also be a source of guidance on alternatives that the child and his family might not have been aware of.

If you can't afford a private counselor, contact your local office of Health and Rehabilitative Services. In most states, they offer counseling free to troubled families. For a chronic runaway they can have a court order issued to go before a judge, who can then order him not to run away. If he does run, the police can pick him up and put him in protective custody. This is a last resort measure, but one that has been effective in many cases.

Running away is difficult to deal with. It isn't a crime. You can't force your child to live with you. Since it is usually a symptom of family conflict, bringing your child back into the same environment he left will only result in his running away again.

DANGERS OF THE STREET

Most runaways — about seven out of ten — never leave their home county; eight out of ten return home on their own within 72 hours.

What had first seemed to the runaway a solution to his problems, a weapon designed to bring his parents around to his way of thinking, becomes, in most cases, an intolerable burden. The child simply has not thought of how he will be provided with food and shelter. He is unprepared for the callousness, indifference and sometimes ruthlessness and cruelty of people on the "outside." The horrifying possibility of losing the only security he knows usually causes an abrupt change in plans.

But the dangers are very real. Many runaways look for thrills in bars and adult movie houses, where they can very easily overstep their boundaries, falling victims to those who literally prey on children and teenagers. And many more, alone and frightened, are easily spotted and quickly tagged as "the new kids."

One thirteen-year-old recalls that she barely arrived in New York's Port Authority before she was approached by a man who was obviously up to no good. Another man and a woman headed him off and offered to take her to their house. Fortunately, the police were there as well,

Home of a runaway, San Francisco, California

and she was soon on a plane headed home. A Philadelphia 16-year-old was not so lucky. She accepted the offer for help and soon found herself pregnant by her newfound "friend." Other runaways, too young to work legally and with no other way to support themselves, end up in such infamous places as New York's Minnesota strip — a mecca for teenage prostitutes — and Hollywood's Santa Monica Boulevard, where boy hookers ply their trade. Others learn to steal or deal drugs.

Most runaways on the streets for more than a month turn to prostitution as the only way to survive. On the average, they remain in it for three years. In most large cities, child prostitution is largely mob controlled, as is child pornography, which also recruits runaways. In Manhattan, runaway children as young as eight or nine are picked up by pimps, beaten, addicted to drugs, and sent out as prostitutes.

Local and national call services and "buy-a-kid" rings sell runaway children for a night or permanently. The cost of buying a child for life can run from $500 to $5,000.

Many runaways — about 150,000 each year — simply disappear. Since they have no health insurance nor access to medical care, disease is rampant. Venereal disease, drug-related disorders, and malnutrition are common, often resulting in death.

The longer the child is on the streets, the less hope there is that he will be found. Father Bruce Ritter, of New York City's Covenant House for runaway youths, says, "If a kid has lived in the streets for a month or so, it is very hard to reach him. If it's been six months, we've almost lost him and if it's a year, he's gone. The poison works very, very quickly."

If your child has run away, it's imperative that you take action immediately.

THE QUEST

With a runaway, follow the same steps as with any missing child. Call his friends. One police officer who has successfully tracked many runaways says that he has located more through their friends than in any other way. Quite often a parent will allow a child's friend to stay at his house, not knowing that the friend is a runaway. And it isn't unusual for a parent to cooperate when his child asks him, "He's having a little trouble at home; can he stay here for a few days?" Some parents truly feel they are helping the child; others simply don't care enough to contact the friend's parents.

Often friends are reluctant to talk and will resolutely maintain that they know nothing. Try to get their cooperation by explaining what a serious situation it could be. If they know where your child has gone and won't give you any information, they may accidentally drop a clue to his whereabouts. Talk to their parents and ask their cooperation by calling you in the event your runaway calls or contacts their children.

To find children who might know your child only casually, and thus are not sworn to secrecy, try his favorite hangout. If you would look or feel out of place, send someone who can fit in better — a brother or sister, or a trusted or well-liked teacher, counselor, or police officer. Because these people have had experience working with young people, they will be better able to talk to them on a street level. They can spend some time rapping with the youngsters and gaining their confidence before asking for information. In many cases, a child who develops a rapport with such a person will take it upon himself to find out for him where the child has gone.

Call the school and talk to the counselor and your child's teachers. Sometimes a child leaves home because of fear of punishment for a bad report card or disciplinary action at school. Also, someone there may know more than you do about your child's activities, his involvement with cliques, gangs, drugs and school friends who may have information.

At some point soon after you have concluded that your child probably left home voluntarily, you should **call the nearest office of the F.B.I., if you haven't already, to verify that your child's name is listed in the**

NCIC computer. If it is not, request it. You may be asked to sign a formal request form in the case of a known runaway, however.

There are other agencies and organizations you can begin contacting, too, such as the Salvation Army's Department of Missing Persons. The American Red Cross has a similar office. There are runaway shelters such as Covenant House in New York City and other places . . . 169 of them funded by the federal government alone. Runaway and crisis hotlines are listed in your telephone book.

Any form of publicity could be helpful in locating your runaway. When 18-year-old Kimberly Zielinski returned to her Florida home after having been missing for two years, it was in response to an article in a weekly tabloid which carried her picture. "We feel that getting pictures before the public is going to do more for parents than all those police reports that go out," her mother remarked.

Kimberly had put off calling home for two years mainly because of what had happened to a friend of hers who had also run away. As Mrs. Zielinski describes it, "When the friend's mother was notified that the police had found her and wanted the mother to pick up her girl, she said, 'No. She's not coming back here.' Kimberly's fear about coming home was based on that experience.

"But when she saw the picture in the paper, she knew we still cared and wanted her."

Kimberly's experience illustrates a very real problem with many runaways—the fear that their parents will be angry with them and will not want them back. It may be necessary to assure the child that the door is open for him.

Make a thorough search of the child's room, or of any

other part of the house where he has been. Look through notebooks, boxes of stationery, letters or notes he has written or received. Check purses and pockets in his clothing. Empty the wastebaskets and look for scraps of paper with names, addresses, telephone numbers. Police will check these out for you.

One mother located her child through a stolen oil company credit card. When she noticed the card was missing, she went to all the nearby service stations that sold that brand of gasoline, with the credit card number and the girl's picture. When the girl drove up, an alert attendant recognized her and called her mother.

Remember that most runaways never leave their own county. Your search has a better chance of success if you stay close to home. An exception to this is the child who goes to join a parent in another city. Always check with the other parent, as well as with siblings living away from home.

Teamster locals are cooperative in putting out bulletins on CB radios in the likely event your child will take to the road. Other sources of assistance are listed in Chapter XII.

It is as important to **put out a poster on a runaway child as for any other disappearance**. Posters are especially effective in the city or cities you think might be the destination of your child—beachfront cities, action spots such as Atlantic City or New York. Send them to police departments, to runaway shelters, as well as to truck stops along likely routes the child would take. By all means send them to the offices of national and regional search organizations in these cities.

A child that wants to get lost and stay lost probably can; millions do every year. Unlike adults, children leave no trail, no public records. They live off the land for weeks at a time, and the contacts they make know them

A runaway's end

only by first name.

But persistence in the search has paid off in many cases. Continue to check with your contacts. Check any and all leads. Keep in touch with the runaway shelters and hotlines that can and frequently do find the child and open broken lines of communication between parent and child. One of the less well-known well-known functions of Child Find, Inc., and similar organizations, is providing a way for children who have been missing from home — whether because of abduction or because they ran away — to get back in touch through an understanding intermediary.

CHAPTER IX

WHEN THE TOUGH GET GOING

There is no price tag on a child.

Senator Paula Hawkins

BACKTRACKING

Hopefully, by the second or third day your child will be found or will have returned home on his own. Or perhaps by this time you at least know where he is and that he is safe.

If the child has not returned by nightfall of the day he disappeared, the odds are still in your favor. Although fears seem to increase with the coming of darkness and imagination begins to work overtime, many a lost child will settle down under a tree or protected spot to await the coming of daylight. Runaways often "crash" at a friend's house overnight and return home in the morning. And law enforcement agencies work around the clock. Often, especially where a child is concerned, they will put in an extra shift and add off-duty officers to help in the search.

After the second or third day, if you still have no word as to your child's whereabouts, you can assume a serious situation exists. With the passing of time, the odds, once overwhelmingly in your favor, diminish greatly. The matter is now firmly in official hands. But your job is not over.

This is an important point, especially if the child was taken by a stranger: **Exactly twenty-four hours after your child's disappearance, return to the place where he disappeared**. There may be regular delivery people, telephone or other utility repair crews or service people who were in the same area the day before when your child disappeared. They might have seen him, or they might have other information useful in your search. Retrace the route your child might have used. Ask everyone you see in the vicinity. You should also check with people who live in homes close to the spot where the child disappeared and with store owners or sales people nearby. Write down what you learn.

Continue to pursue the clues you have. Call your child's friends again. They might have heard something by now or remember something they had not mentioned before.

Continue to search your memory. You may think of other people you can call, other places you can look.

If as much as a week—or even two or three days—has passed, **contact one of the national, regional or local search organizations** that deal with missing children. Their names and addresses are in Chapter XII. You should have written them on your **Child-Pac Datacards** and in your **Parents Action Plan**, too. Given them the facts from the **Child-Pac Datacards** and tell them what you have done and what you have learned. Also contact:

* The State Highway Patrol—for highway traffic and hitchhiking violation arrests

* Truckers' associations—for possible reports of hitchhikers or CB broadcasts which might have given information

* Armed forces recruiting centers.

THE PRESS CONFERENCE

It is now time to call a press conference with the assistance of the police. Structure it carefully, and make it brief. Its purpose is to get your child's description and the circumstances of the disappearance to the thousands or hundreds of thousands who will be seeing it on the evening newscast or reading about it in the paper.

Prepare in advance what you will say. Write it down; the emotion of the moment may make it difficult to keep your mind on what you want to say. Don't worry about showing emotion, though. It will convey the full impact of your loss to others and make it real to those whose help you need and want.

Ask for and get the full cooperation and assistance of media personnel. Media involvement now will force police to stay on the case, even though they think the trail is cold.

You should also **go to the full printing of your poster** at this time—1,000 or more copies. Post them in shopping centers, schools, at playgrounds and in hospital emergency rooms. Give copies to people who work in these places. You might want to mail some out of town, if you have an idea of where your child might have gone. Post them anywhere you think they will be seen by someone who can help you.

As a last resort, contact area morgues for bodies of unidentified children. An agency which can give information on possible deaths is the Bergen County (New Jersey) Missing Persons Bureau. Contact Sgt. Dick Ruffino. Bergen County maintains a file on the unidentified bodies. The address and telephone number are listed in Chapter XII. NCIC plans in the near future to match the descriptions of missing persons with unidentified body information at such centers and at morgues across the country.

By this time you will have done most of what you can do until the official investigation turns up something else. Your child's name and vital information are in the NCIC computer, and the information will be carried across the country. The F.B.I. will be working across state lines. Relax, as much as you can, and continue to search your memory for clues.

With a missing child, everyone who has had close contact with him will be suspect—including his parents. Very personal questions will probably be asked. If your first reaction is anger or resentment, remember the questions are intended only to get the facts and to help find and bring your child home sooner. Be honest, open and thorough in sharing your information and knowledge. It could pay off in a speedier recovery.

A final comment . . . the police and the F.B.I. are part of a system, the criminal justice system. But, however well organized, the system won't work if you don't work with it. If you find your child after he has been reported missing to the police, the F.B.I. and private search agencies, notify them, so they can clear the case and have more time for other missing children.

CHAPTER X

RECOVERY

*You have never been young in the world I am
young in, and you never can be . . .*

Margaret Mead

LOOKING TOWARD TOMORROW

Your child has been recovered — hopefully alive and unharmed. The feeling of relief is enormous — probably greater than you have ever known or will ever know again. You eagerly look forward to getting on with the regular routine of your life.

But it's never that easy. Getting lost or abducted — even in the mildest of cases — is a trauma, and must be dealt with as such. Even if your child was not physically harmed or threatened by anyone and was returned to you in a very short time, he has known the terror of being away from home and familiar surroundings. He probably feared the worst — even if it didn't happen. He wonders if he can ever again feel really safe.

Your first step in securing the right type of psychological counseling will probably be to talk with your minister or family doctor. Depending on the circumstances, including your financial situation, he will suggest a qualified psychiatrist or psychologist, or refer you to a mental health center or family agency with trained professionals who will work with you. If you find it difficult to pay for a private counselor, he will probably know of agencies who work on a "sliding scale," with fees proportionate to your family's income.

Counseling is important for everyone in the family. Parents, brothers and sisters need to know how to deal with the problem. Often they will need help in their relationship to the child who was missing — what to say to him, how to help him adjust. Group counseling with other families might also be suggested to you. When choosing a counselor, keep in mind that many have little experience in this area. Find out if this person has worked with cases of child abduction before, and what his reputation is. Ask former clients. If a counselor tells you that your child is too young, or that he will need only a few sessions to recover, find another counselor.

Your community might have **support groups** of families who have gone through this type of experience. Or you might want to start such a group. Interaction with others who have "been there" can be invaluable in dealing with problems of adjustment. You'll find a healthy exchange of ideas on what to do, how to handle emotions and problems of adjustment. You'll also find comfort in knowing that you are not alone, that there are others who care and can empathize with you.

Parental abduction can be as traumatic as any other kind. In many cases a child has adjusted to a whole new way of life and may not even remember his custodial parent when he is returned. He may have been told very disturbing things about the parent who stayed at home and learned other disturbing things about the parent who abducted him, including the fact that his motive was spite or revenge, not the child's welfare. In any case, he is probably confused and may have formed a whole new set of value judgments.

If the child was mistreated or threatened, his problem is even more severe. If he was raped or severely molested, he may need months or years of professional counseling to be able to cope with the problem and learn to go on living.

Reactions vary, but symptoms can include nightmares, shyness, depression, nervousness, anxiety, and tension. One child, for more than a year after she had been abducted and locked in a box, woke up screaming, with the feeling she was being suffocated. Another, kidnapped by a bearded stranger, became hysterical when she saw a man with a beard. Many children feel an irrational sense of guilt, as if they were somehow to blame for what happened. Some show no outward reactions immediately afterward, but weeks, months, or even several years later experience post traumatic shock, similar to the reaction of many combat veterans.

If the worst should happen, if the child isn't found and returned, life afterward for the family is frequently grief without end. . .without the final acceptance because there is no true final reality. Psychological counseling may be a lifesaving necessity. Neighbors, old friends often will not know what to say and after a while will stop trying. They may quietly suspect that the parents had something to do with the disappearance — through neglect or some action. Others, especially younger children in the family, may be worried about its happening to them. Parents may blame themselves for things they might have done or not done to prevent its happening. An empty bed, a vacant place at the dinner table, an unused tennis racket or baseball glove — all kinds of reminders—constantly make everyone in the family painfully aware of the new "unbalanced" family structure. Younger brothers and sisters especially will have difficulty understanding and coping with the new, harsh reality.

Getting back into the routine is essential. So is the love and understanding of neighbors, friends and family. The support groups mentioned earlier may be a very important link to the return to normal life. In any event, you don't have to go it alone.

There are no words to say what to do if your child is found dead. Nature alone has answers. As in other cases, counseling by a mental health professional or clergyman and the fellowship of a support group could be invaluable.

John and Reve Walsh have been an inspiration to many. So have Betty and Ivana DiNova, Gloria and Ray Yerkovich, Stan and Julie Patz, Jim DeGray and

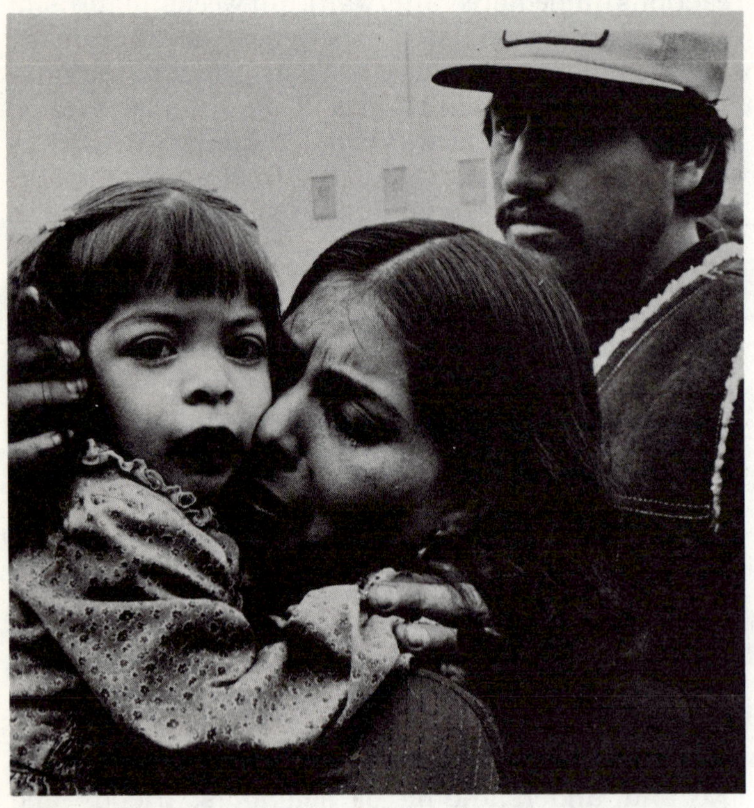

Lucretia Martinez is reunited with her parents in Salinas, California.

Margaret Strickland, all of whom have experienced the loss of their own child or one closely related to them. Perhaps you, like them, could turn your loss into a victory for children, someday. . .by working in the community with organizations like the Walsh Foundation, the Dee Scofield Awareness Program, and Child Find, Inc. to save other children from tragedy and other families from heartbreak.

CHAPTER XI

INVOLVING THE COMMUNITY

*Natural rights exist
even for children, and
it is their right not to
be corrupted, nor to be
deceived, nor to be led astray.*

Massimo d'Azeglio

JOINING HANDS

Julie Patz, the mother we talked about earlier, didn't learn of her son Etan's early morning disappearance until 3:40 p.m. because his school didn't call to tell her he hadn't arrived.

There were reasons. A school bus drivers' strike had just ended, and the schedule was in chaos. That morning the bus arrived ten minutes early. The other children had already been picked up and the parents gone home when Etan arrived at his stop.

It was a simple breakdown in communications — with tragic results.

The writing of this book involved hours of reading and research. The authors talked to many people who had been directly involved with missing children, including parents, some of whom had recovered their children and others who had not. From all of the interviews and research, the need for strong community involvement became startlingly apparent. Because of the epidemic nature of the problem, individual and family action is simply not enough. Schools, churches, civic organizations, city and county governments — all need to be educated as to the seriousness of the situation and to get to work on helping to find solutions.

IN THE SCHOOLS

The P.T.A. (or other parent organization at your school) can be a powerful force in making positive changes. But it is only as strong as the individuals who comprise it. **Get involved**, and contact other parents to get involved also. Use it as a forum to get out information on the problem and the dangers involved.

Through the P.T.A., **push for a standard policy**

requiring the school office to call any parent whose child does not appear at school. If you hear the argument that there is no time or money for this, organize a volunteer program composed of parents or senior citizens. Contact your local senior center or chapter of The American Association of Retired Persons (AARP). Many communities have had success with senior volunteer programs.

Volunteers could also help on school buses. Again using the P.T.A., get the school board to **require a passenger manifest on all buses, listing each child who boards each time.** Or names could be checked off on a prepared list. Have your volunteers ready so that you can again counter the argument of lack of time or money.

What are the student registration requirements at your school? **Schools should insist on documentation of the custody of each child,** just as they do on immunizations. A year-to-year photographic record of the child should be kept to support continuity of custody. If a parent alleges the other parent is dead, the school should ask for a copy of the death certificate.

Through your P.T.A. or similar organization, **talk up awareness.** Schedule programs for both parents and children. Many excellent films, pamphlets, books and potential speakers are available through the organizations listed in Chapter XII.

Through your P.T.A. or city or county juvenile justice system, push to see that any school or other organization which works with children or youth be required to make a **thorough background check on every employee.** See that a voluntary "Waiver of the Right to Privacy" be made a condition of employment for every worker, paid or unpaid.

As John Rabun, manager of the Jefferson County

(Kentucky) Missing Child Unit, told a U.S. Senate Sub-committee on Juvenile Justice, "We go about hiring people and placing them in very sensitive positions because they say they like kids. The whole definition of pedophilia is an attraction to kids, so that should not be the definition for hiring people to work in children's programs."

Parents are not the only people with misconceptions about the identity of child molesters. More and more cases are coming to light of respected, trusted youth workers exploiting youngsters by taking advantage of their position of trust. Crimes run from fondling, to securing children for highly organized rings of prostitution and child porn, to rape and murder. It is imperative that not only schools but organizations such as Boy and Girl Scouts, Big Brothers and Big Sisters, and church and community youth groups take greater care in screening prospective employees.

You are only asking these organizations to do for the security of our children what banks routinely do for the security of our money.

As a starting effort to get your P.T.A. or other organization involved and to increase awareness, **get a child fingerprinting effort going in your community.** Do it every year. . . perhaps at school registration. Better yet, tell other parents and the P.T.A. about the newly developed five-part **Child-Safe Program**, which consists of:

> *   *My Child Is Not Missing: A Parents Guide Book.* A comprehensive resource book to instruct parents of the preventive measures necessary to avoid child abduction, and a step-by-step recovery system for missing children (e.g., runaways, parental kidnapping, criminal abductions).

* **Child-Pac Datacards:**™ A highly detailed information and identification file on your child, containing items of vital importance: fingerprints, photos, body charts, dental records, hair and fingernail analysis samples, handwriting examples, school information, etc., which will assist you and the authorities in the quick recovery of your missing child.

* **Parents Action Plan:**™ A pre-planned methodical search system which helps to avoid the confusion and memory lapses which occur and cost precious time when it counts most . . . if your child is missing.

* **Break Away/Get Away Video Tapes:** (prepared under the directorship of Joe Hess, Police Academy Supervisor for Survival Training). A comprehensive video tape production to train your child in the most effective ways of eluding the grasps of child abductors. (Available in BETA and VHS)

* **Stranger Danger Audio Cassette Tapes:** Educational and entertaining audio cassette tapes geared primarily for children. These tapes will bring awareness to and instruct youngsters of all ages of the potentially hazardous situations in which child abduction most frequently occurs.

For additional information, call Child Safe Products, Inc., at:

Outside Florida: 1-800-334-0090
Florida Residents: (305) 472-6070

If the leaders in your city or county government are not doing something about the problem of missing children, it is up to you and other concerned citizens to insist that they begin.

The problem is so widespread today that no matter where you live you can find "horror stories" about child abduction in your area or one close by. Just search the files at the office of your local newspaper. Make copies of the stories you find — so you will have plenty of ammunition for those who underestimate the frequency and scope of the problem. It is one that involves everyone.

Talk to the mayor and city council about your concerns. Do some research before you go, so that you will have some suggestions for things the community can do. Get city officials to commit themselves to an "Action Program to Safeguard Our Kids." You could suggest that the mayor, through a resolution of the city council, proclaim a "Safeguard Our Kids" week. During the week the city could launch a **Safe Homes Program** as a part of Neighborhood Watch, where one home on each block is marked with a colorful, conspicuous decal which designates it as a haven for any child who is lost or needs help.

Be sure that anyone who participates in such a program is carefully checked out. Do a background check just as we suggested on others that have regular contact with your children. This program has operated very successfully in many communities. Write to the National Association for Missing Children for information on how to organize it.

Talk to the chief of police or sheriff about NCIC, and ask how often it has been used. Find out what they do in the event a child is reported missing.

The NCIC's computer can be a powerful instrument, but the public needs to be made aware that it is available. Its use is voluntary, and a survey made for the Congressional hearings on the Missing Children's Act revealed that only 10 to 14% of missing children had been reported to NCIC.

Together with the mayor or juvenile authorities, suggest that an **action group** be formed, similar to the Kentucky Task Force on Exploited and Missing Children in Louisville, Kentucky. The address is listed in Chapter XII. Write to them for information on how to organize this type of committee.

While you're talking with community officials, find out if security officers in shopping malls and other public places are licensed by the state or local government. Check to see that they have had training on how to deal with cases of missing children and that they have a definite plan of action if a child is lost, including calling in the police if the child is not found within a half hour.

Find out from the police chief if he has a program for training volunteers to work as search teams in the event a child is ever missing in your community. If not, see that such a program is begun.

Some states are making their own efforts at recovery of missing children. The state of Florida, spurred by the efforts of John and Reve Walsh and others, has a computerized file and a hotline parents can use to get their missing child's information into "the system." Florida state law also requires the police to enter reports on missing children immediately, not twenty-four hours later. What laws and programs does your state have? Remember, it was only through parents like the Walshs, who wouldn't give up, that things changed.

IN THE COURTS

Family mediation is coming to be used more and more to "cool down" the disputes that frequently erupt around property settlement and child custody in divorce cases. Cooling the issues and defining parental rights and responsibilities can probably prevent parental abduction with its anguish and pain. Check to find out the attitude and practice of the courts in your community and state. Does the law encourage or even require mediation? How can it be made a part of your legal system? Check with your local and state bar association and get some action started.

Another question related to parental kidnapping: In your community, is **temporary custody** usually or occasionally given prior to a final property settlement and divorce decree? Could it be made a required part of divorce filing procedures? Again, your local and state bar association can be a source of information and assistance.

IN YOUR NEIGHBORHOOD AND COMMUNITY

Join or **start a support group** for parents who have gone through the experience and for those who want to know how they can prevent it. A great deal can come out of the interaction—an end to feelings of isolation and alienation, a sharing of feelings, of ways and means of recovering missing children and preventing their becoming missing in the first place, of working with the media, the schools and police. It's a way of staying involved, together.

These suggestions are just for starters. You will think of other steps you can take, particularly as you work with other parents.

The strength of our nation is built on the strength of

the smallest unit. Your little community group can build into a city, county or statewide network working with other networks in other cities and states. The result will be a stronger voice in Congress and better legislation and judicial processes.

REVIEW

*   Does the office at your child's school routinely call any parent whose child does not appear at school?

*   Do school buses have a passenger manifest, listing all passengers and the times they board?

*   Does your child's school have educational programs on child safety for both children and parents?

*   Do all organizations in your community that work with children require background checks of all employees and volunteer workers.

*   Have you talked to your city officials about community programs for child safety?

*   Is the NCIC computer being used in your community?

*   Are security officers in shopping malls and other public places licensed by state or local government?

*   Does your police chief have a program for training volunteers to search for missing children?

*   Does the court system in your area have a program for family mediation for domestic problems?

*   Do the courts have a policy of granting temporary custody of children whose parents are involved in divorce action?

*   Does your community have a support group for parents who have had a child missing?

CHAPTER XII

WHERE TO TURN

*There is no limit to what can be
accomplished if one doesn't care
who gets credit for it . . .*

John Clinkscales

The following listing of organizations is by no means a listing of all organizations involved with the tragedy of missing children. It includes those that have appeared in several sources over the past year, have some prior listing of activity and are known to several of the larger, stronger organizations. Many have responded to a recent questionnaire on their status and activities sent by the National Association for Missing Children.

There may be many not listed which are excellent and which should be included. We hope our readers will provide us with information on them so that they can be included in the next edition of the *Parents Guide Book.*

Listing does not constitute an endorsement of the agency or group listed.

MISSING CHILDREN'S AGENCY DIRECTORY

ALABAMA

Division of Child Support Activities
    Mr. Paul Vincent, Director
    Bureau of Public Assistance
    State Department of Pensions and Security
    64 North Union Street
    Montgomery, Alabama 36130
    (205) 261-2872

ALASKA

Child Support Enforcement Agency
    Mr. Dan Copeland, Director
    Department of Revenue
    201 East 9th Avenue, Room 202
    Anchorage, Alaska 99501
    (907) 276-3441

Hide and Seek of Fairbanks
    Robert and Julie Parzick
    SR Box 80292
    Fairbanks, Alaska 99701
    (907) 488-3591
(See Hide and Seek, Inc. Oregon)

Missing Children of America, Inc.
    Nancy Barros, Director
    P.O. Box 1938
    Anchorage, Alaska
    (907) 243-8484/272-8484

Suicide Prevention and Crisis
    P.O. Box 2863
    Anchorage, Alaska 99510
    (907) 276-1600 HOTLINE
    (907) 279-0333 HOTLINE
    (907) 272-2496

ARIZONA

Child Support Enforcement Administration
    Mr. John Ahl, Program Administrator
    Department of Economic Security
    P.O. Box 6123 - Site Code 966C
    Phoenix, Arizona 85005
    (602) 255-3465

ARKANSAS

Office of Child Support Enforcement
    Mr. Ed Baskin, Acting Director
    Arkansas Social Services
    P.O. Box 3358
    Little Rock, Arkansas 72203
    (501) 371-2464

CALIFORNIA

Bay Area Center for Victims of Child Stealing
    Georgia Hilgeman, Executive Director
    1165 Meridian Avenue, #118
    San Jose, California 95125
    (408) 247-0195/723-7804/270-2133 (Hayward)
    (707) 544-6536 (Santa Rosa)

Center for the Family in Transition
Child Stealing Project
    Dr. Dorothy Huntington
    Barry Feinberg
    5725 Paradise Drive, Bldg. A, Suite 100
    Corte Madera, California 94925
    (415) 924-5750

Find the Children, Inc.
    Linda Otto
    11811 W. Olympic Boulevard
    Los Angeles, California 90064
    (213) 477-6721

Freedom Counseling Center
    Lowell D. Streiker, Executive Director
    1633 Old Bayshore Highway, Suite 265
    Burlingame, California 94010
    (415) 692-1403

Missing Teens & Young Adults
    Ms. Eileen Luboff
    P.O. Box 7800
    Santa Cruz, California 95061
    (408) 425-3663 HOTLINE

National "Kid Print" Program
    Chief G. M. Stockdale
    P.O. Box 5548
    Buena Park, California 90622
    (714) 778-0375

Sacramento Stolen Children Action Network
    2103 Stockton Boulevard
    Sacramento, California 95817
    (916) 453-0713

CANADA

The Tania Murrell Missing Children Society
    Mr. & Mrs. Jack Murrell
    9913 151 Ar.
    Edmonton, Alberta T5P 1T2
    (403) 486-7777

Operation Go-Home
    Reverend Norman Johnston
    P.O. Box 12
    Westport, Ontario K0G 1X9
    (613) 273-2046

COLORADO

Division of Child Support Enforcement
    Mr. James O. Galeotti, Director
    Department of Social Services
    1575 Sherman Street - Room 517
    Denver, Colorado 80203
    (303) 866-2422
    (303) 866-5000 General Information

CONNECTICUT

Child Support Division
    Mr. Anthony DiNallo, Chief
    Department of Human Resources
    110 Bartholemew Avenue
    Hartford, Connecticut 06106
    (203) 566-3053

DELAWARE

Bureau of Child Support Enforcement
    Mr. Rick Bennett, Director
    Department of Health & Social Services
    P.O. Box 904
    Newcastle, Delaware 19720
    (302) 571-3620

DISTRICT OF COLUMBIA

American Bar Association
National Resource Center for
Child Advocacy and Protection
    Howard Davidson, Director
    1800 M Street, N.W.
    Washington, D.C. 20036
    (202) 331-2250

Bureau of Paternity
    Mr. Eugene Brown, Chief
    Child Support Enforcement
    Department of Human Services
    425 I Street N.W.
    Washington, D.C. 20004
    (202) 724-5610

HALT
201 Massachusetts Avenue N.E.
Suite 319
Washington, D.C. 20002
(202) 546-4258

FLORIDA

Abducted Children Information Center
Harvey Morse
1470 Gene Street
Winter Park, Florida 32789
(305) 831-2000

Adam Walsh Child Resource Center
Denny Abbott, Executive Director
1876 N. University Drive, #306
Fort Lauderdale, Florida 33322
(305) 475-4847

American Federation of Police Child Guard Center
Col. Lyman P. Davison, President
1100 N.E. 125th Street
North Miami, Florida 33161
(305) 891-1700

Children's Rights of Florida, Inc.
Kathy Rosenthall, President
P.O. Box 173
Pinellas Park, Florida 33565
(813) 546-1593 HOTLINE

Dee Scofield Awareness Program
Betty DiNova
4418 Bay Court Avenue
Tampa, Florida 33611
(813) 839-5025 HOTLINE

James DeGray Foundation for Missing Children
    2927 Ramada Drive, Apt. 431
    Tampa, Florida 33612
    (813) 977-9174

Loaned Angels, Inc.
    Ms. Kathleen Mancil
    P.O. Box 888
    Hernando, Florida 32642
    (904) 726-0999

Missing Children Help Center
    Ivanna DiNova
    410 Ware Boulevard
    Tampa, Florida 33619
    (813) 681-HELP
    (813) 623-KIDS

Missing Persons Nationwide, Inc.
    Alfie Brisben
    P.O. Box 5331
    Hudson, Florida 33568
    (813) 856-5144

National Association for Missing Children, Inc.
    Martin Fierro, Director
    300 South University Drive
    Plantation, Florida 33324
    (305) 473-6126

National Children's Fingerprint Bank
    Kenneth Campbell
    P.O. Box 3737, 1445 Second Street
    Sarasota, Florida 33577
    (813) 366-4669

Office of Child Support Enforcement
    Mr. Samuel G. Ashdown, Jr., Director
    Department of Health & Rehabilitative Services
    1317 Winewood Boulevard
    Tallahassee, Florida 32301
    (904) 488-9900

Parents Helping Parents
    Cindy Teel
    Rt. 1, Box 406D
    Myakka, Florida 33551
    (813) 322-1918

Safe House, Inc.
    Al Palmquist, Director
    Norman Parchette, Assistant Director
    1058 Sunset Point Road
    Clearwater, Florida 33515
    (813) 446-5529

GEORGIA

C.E.F.M.
    P.O. Box 82664
    Atlanta, Georgia 30354
    (404) 233-8630
    (518) 756-8014 (New York)

Child Support Recovery Unit
    Mr. Jesse Beck, Director
    State Department of Human Resources
    878 Peachtree Street, N.E. Room 529
    Atlanta, Georgia 30309
    (404) 894-5194

Find Me, Inc.
    John and Louise Clinkscales
    P.O. Box 1612
    La Grange, Georgia 30241
    (404) 884-7419
    (See next item)

Kyle's Story
    John Clinkscales
    205 N. Chilton Avenue
    La Grange, Georgia 30240

Parents Against Child Snatching
    Kimberly Willis
    5311A Williams Road
    Norcross, Georgia 30093
    (412) 264-9025

HAWAII

Child Support Enforcement Agency
    Mr. James O'Brien, IV-D Administrator
    770 Kapiolani Boulevard, Suite 403
    Honolulu, Hawaii 96813
    (808) 548-6773

IDAHO

Child Protection
    Mrs. Pat Barrell, Chief
    Department of Health and Welfare
    1105 South Orchard
    Boise, Idaho 83705
    (208) 338-7100

ILLINOIS

Bureau of Child Support
    Mr. Gerald D. Slavens, Chief
    Department of Public Aid
    316 South Second Street
    Springfield, Illinois 62762
    (217) 782-1366

National Runaway Switchboard
    2210 North Halsted
    Chicago, Illinois 60614
    1-800-972-6004 HOTLINE (Illinois)
    1-800-231-6946 HOTLINE

INDIANA

Child Support Enforcement Division
    Mr. Thomas W. McKean, Director
    State Department of Public Welfare
    141 South Meridian Street, 4th Floor
    Indianapolis, Indiana 46225
    (317) 232-4903

IOWA

Child Support Recovery Unit
    Mr. Jack Baughman, Director
    Iowa Department of Social Services
    Hoover Building - 5th Floor
    Des Moines, Iowa 50319
    (515) 281-5580

KANSAS

Location and Support
    Ms. Betty Hummel, Director
    Dept. of Social & Rehabilitation Services
    2700 West 6th - Perry Building
    Topeka, Kansas 66606
    (913) 296-4188

Parents Alone
    Mary Anne Havey
    Wichita State University
    Dept. of Psychology
    Box 34
    Wichita, Kansas 67208
    (316) 689-3170

KENTUCKY

Division of Child Support Enforcement
    Mr. Hanson Williams, Director
    Bureau of Social Insurance
    Department of Human Resources
    275 East Main Street, 6th Floor
    Frankfort, Kentucky 40621
    (502) 564-2285

E.C.H.O. (Exploited Children's Help Organization)
    Rosie Norris
    1204 South 3rd Street, Suite B
    Louisville, Kentucky 40203
    (502) 637-8761

Kentucky Alliance for Exploited
and Missing Children, Inc.
    Ron Pregliasco
    400 South 6th Street, 3rd Floor
    Louisville, Kentucky 40202
    (502) 581-5787

Kentucky Task Force on Exploited
and Missing Children
    609 West Jefferson Street
    Louisville, Kentucky 40202
    (502) 587-3621

LOUISIANA

Support Enforcement Services
    Mr. P.M. Blakney, Director
    P.O. Box 44276
    Baton Rouge, Louisiana 70804
    (504) 342-4780

Young Americans
    Daniel Villaurbia
    P.O. Box 59672
    New Orleans, Louisiana 70156
    (504) 467-0700

MAINE

Coalition Organized for Parental Equality
    Peter T. Cyr
    68 Deering Street
    Portland, Maine 04101
    (207) 775-0258

Support Enforcement and Location Unit
    Mr. Colburn Jackson, Director
    Bureau of Social Welfare
    Department of Human Services
    State House, Station 11
    Augusta, Maine 04333
    (207) 289-2886

MARYLAND

Child Support Enforcement Administration
    Mr. John Williams, Chief
    Income Maintenance Administration
    300 West Preston Street, 5th Floor
    Baltimore, Maryland 21201
    (301) 576-5389

Mothers Without Custody, Inc.
    P.O. Box 602
    Riverdale, Maryland 20770
    (301) 345-5911

MASSACHUSETTS

Child Support Enforcement Unit
    Mr. Dennis Sullivan, Director
    Department of Public Welfare
    600 Washington Street
    Boston, Massachusetts 02111
    (617) 727-7820

Childsearch
    Robert Cohen
    6 Beacon Street, Suite 600
    Boston, Massachusetts 02108
    (617) 720-1760

MICHIGAN

Fathers for Equal Rights
    Leigh Travis
    861 Honey Creek Road
    Ann Arbor, Michigan 48103
    (313) 761-3427

H.E.A.R.T. (Help Every Abduction Return Today)
    Leslie Campbell
    10937 Red Arrow Highway
    Route 1
    Mattawan, Michigan 59071
    (616) 668-3733

Office of Child Support
    Mr. Jerrold Brockmyre, Director
    Department of Social Services
    300 South Capitol Avenue - Suite 621
    Lansing, Michigan 48933
    (517) 373-7570

Searching Parents Association
    Susan Humphrey, Director
    P.O. Box 582
    East Tawas, Michigan 48730
    (517) 362-7148

MINNESOTA

Office of Child Support
    Mrs. Bonnie Becker, Director
    Department of Public Welfare
    Space Center Building
    444 Lafayette Road
    St. Paul, Minnesota 55101
    (612) 296-2499

MISSISSIPPI

Child Support Division
    Mr. Monte L. Barton, Director
    State Department of Public Welfare
    P.O. Box 352
    Jackson, Mississippi 39205
    (601) 354-0341, Ext. 503

MISSOURI

Child Support Enforcement Unit
    Mr. Paul Nelson, Administrator
    Division of Family Services
    Department of Social Services
    P.O. Box 88
    Jefferson City, Missouri 65103
    (314) 751-4301

MONTANA

Child Support Enforcement Bureau
    Mr. Ray Linder, Bureau Chief
    Montana Department of Revenue
    P.O. Box 5955
    Helena, Montana 59604
    (406) 444-4614

Friends of Child Find (Of Montana)
    Joyce J. Kenney
    725 South Billings Boulevard, No. 0
    Billings, Montana 59101
    (406) 259-6999

NEVADA

Child Support Enforcement Office
    Mr. William Furlong, Chief
    Nevada State Welfare Division
    Department of Human Resources
    430 Jeanell Drive
    Carson City, Nevada 89710
    (702) 885-4744

NEW HAMPSHIRE

Office of Child Support Enforcement Services
    Mr. G. E. Thorn, Administrator
    Division of Welfare
    Health and Welfare Building
    Hazen Drive
    Concord, New Hampshire 03301
    (603) 271-4426

NEW JERSEY

Bergen County New Jersey
Missing Persons Bureau
    Sergeant Dick Ruffino
    1 Court Street
    Hackensack, New Jersey 07601
    (201) 646-2192

Child Support and Paternity Unit
    Mr. Harry Wiggins, Chief
    Department of Human Services
    P.O. Box CN 716
    Trenton, New Jersey 08625
    (609) 633-6000

Hide and Seek of Camden, N.J.
    Jim and Nikki Thoman
    150 Berlin Road
    Gibbsboro, New Jersey 08026
    (609) 783-3101
(See Hide and Seek, Inc. Oregon)

Search
    Charles Sutherland
    560 Sylvan Avenue
    Englewood Cliffs, New Jersey 07632
    (201) 567-4040

NEW MEXICO

Child Support Enforcement Bureau
    Mr. Ben Silva, Chief
    Department of Human Services
    P.O. Box 2348 - PERA Building
    Santa Fe, New Mexico 87503
    (505) 827-4230

NEW YORK

Child Find, Inc.
    Gloria Yerkovich
    P.O. Box 277
    New Paltz, New York 12561
    1-800-431-5005 HOTLINE
    (914) 255-1848

Children's Rights of New York, Inc.
    John Gill
    19 Maple Avenue
    Stonybrook, New York 11790
    (516) 751-7840 HOTLINE

Committee to Find Etan Patz
   Ms. Julie Patz
   113 Prince Street
   New York, New York 10012
   (212) 777-3683

Covenant House
   460 West 41st Street
   New York, New York 10036
   (212) 354-4323

Office of Child Support Enforcement
   Mr. Meldon F. Kelsey, Director
   New York State Department of Social Services
   40 North Pearl Street
   Albany, New York 12243
   (518) 474-9081

The Salvation Army Missing Persons Bureau
   120 West 14th Street
   New York, New York 10011
   (212) 620-4362

NORTH CAROLINA

Child Support Enforcement Section
   Ms. Susan Jeffries, Chief
   Division of Social Services
   Department of Human Resources
   443 North Harrington Street
   Raleigh, North Carolina 27603
   (919) 733-4120

NORTH DAKOTA

Department of Human Services
    Mr. Thomas C. Tupa, Administrator
    State Capitol
    Bismarck, North Dakota 58505
    (701) 224-3582

OHIO

Bureau of Child Support
    Mr. Michael Seidemann, Chief
    Department of Public Welfare
    State Office Tower
    30 East Broad Street - 31st Floor
    Columbus, Ohio 43215
    (614) 466-3233

Cobra Connection
    Don Bennafield
    P.O. Box 7016 Station A
    Canton, Ohio 44705
    (216) 454-9109

Parents of Murdered Children
    Charlotte Hullinger
    1739 Bella Vista
    Cincinnati, Ohio 45237
    (513) 721-5683
    (513) 242-8025

OKLAHOMA

Department of Human Services
    Mr. Robert Fulton, Director
    Division of Child Support
    P.O. Box 25352
    Oklahoma City, Oklahoma 73125
    (405) 424-5871

National Child Search, Inc.
    Pearla Kinsey-Peterson
    P.O. Box 800038
    Oklahoma City, Oklahoma 73180
    (405) 685-5621

Friends of Child Find Oklahoma
    Robin Gunning
    P.O. Box 1063
    Choctaw, Oklahoma 73020
    (See Child Find, Inc.)

Oklahoma's Abducted Children, Inc.
    Dean O'Donnell
    P.O. Box 21326
    Oklahoma City, Oklahoma 73120
    (405) 842-7293

Oklahoma Parents Against Child Stealing
    J.C. & Angela Kincaid
    P.O. Box 2112
    Bartlesville, Oklahoma 74005
    (918) 534-1489

OREGON

Hide and Seek Foundation, Inc.
    Linda and Ernie Rivers
    P.O. Box 806
    McMinnville, Oregon 97218
    (503) 472-4333 HOTLINE
    (503) 662-3620

National Missing Children Locate Center, Inc.
    John Bennett, Director
    1123 S.W. Yamhill Street
    Portland, Oregon 97205
    (503) 238-1350

Searching Parents
    Darien S. Fenn
    P.O. Box 19609
    Portland, Oregon 97219
    (503) 246-0573

Support Service
    Mr. Leonard T. Sytsma, Manager
    Department of Human Resources
    P.O. Box 14506
    Salem, Oregon 97310
    (503) 387-6093

PENNSYLVANIA

Child Support Programs
    Ms. Linda Gunn, Director
    Bureau of Claim Settlement
    Department of Public Welfare
    P.O. Box 8018
    Harrisburg, Pennsylvania 17105
    (717) 783-1779

Children's Rights of Pennsylvania, Inc.
    P.O. Box 2764
    Lehigh Valley, Pennsylvania 18001
    (215) 437-2971
    (See Children's Rights of N.Y.)

Hide and Seek of Pennsylvania
    Mike and Barbette Burd
    c/o Woodward Caves
    Woodward, Pennsylvania 16882
    (814) 349-5185
    (See Hide and Seek, Inc. Oregon)

Parents Against Child Snatching (PALS)
    Donna Hodge, President
    P.O. Box 581
    Coropolis, Pennsylvania 15108
    (412) 264-9025 (HOTLINE)
    (412) 526-5537

RHODE ISLAND

Bureau of Family Support
    Mr. George Moriarty, Chief Supervisor
    Dept. of Social & Rehabilitative Services
    77 Dorance Street
    Providence, Rhode Island 02903
    (401) 277-2409

Society for Young Victims
    June Vlasaty
    29 Thurston Avenue
    Newport, Rhode Island 02840
    (401) 847-5083

SOUTH CAROLINA

Division of Child Support
 Mr. Roy T. Loyd, Director
 Public Assistance Division
 Bureau of Public Assistance
  & Field Operations
 Department of Social Services
 P.O. Box 1520
 Columbia, South Carolina 29202
 (803) 758-3151

SOUTH DAKOTA

Office of Child Support Enforcement
 Mr. Leland E. Swann, Program Administrator
 700 Illinois Street
 Pierre, South Dakota 57501
 (605) 773-3641

TENNESSEE

Child Support Services
 Ms. Julia Alexander, Director
 Legal Services Division
 Department of Human Services
 111-19 7th Avenue North, 5th Floor
 Nashville, Tennessee 37203
 (615) 741-3288

TEXAS

Child Support Enforcement Branch
 Mr. Barry Fredrickson, Assistant Commissioner
 Department of Human Resources
 P.O. Box 12548
 Austin, Texas 78711
 (512) 475-0990

Operation Peace of Mind
    P.O. Box 52806
    Houston, Texas 77052
    1-800-392-3352 HOTLINE TEXAS
    1-800-231-6946 HOTLINE NATIONAL

Nation Wide Missing Persons Bureau
    Mildred Stoerner
    3500 Aldine Bender, Box A
    Houston, Texas 77032
    (713) 449-0355

UTAH

Child Find, Inc. - Utah
    Arthur Brogli
    1009 East 4555 South
    Salt Lake City, Utah 84117
    (801) 262-8056   (801) 268-1949

Office of Recovery Services
    Mr. John P. Abbott, Director
    Department of Social Services
    P.O. Box 1500
    Salt Lake City, Utah 84115
    (801) 486-1812

VERMONT

Child Support Division
    Mr. Paul Ohlson, Director
    Department of Social Welfare
    103 South Main Street
    Waterbury, Vermont 05676
    (802) 241-2868

National Coalition for Child Justice
    Ken Wooden
    2998 Shelbourne Road
    Shelbourne, Vermont 05482
    (802) 985-8458

VIRGINIA

Division of Support Enforcement
    Ms. Jean White, Director
    Department of Welfare
    8004 Franklin Farms Drive
    Richmond, Virginia 23288
    (804) 281-9108

WASHINGTON

Families & Friends of Missing Persons
and Violent Crime Victims
    Linda Barker, President
    Jane Addams Bldg.
    11051 34th Avenue, N.E.
    Seattle, Washington 98125
    (206) 362-1081 HOTLINE

Office of Support Enforcement
    Mr. Robert Querry, Chief
    Department of Social & Health Services
    P.O. Box 9162-FU-11
    Olympia, Washington 98504
    (206) 459-6481

WEST VIRGINIA

Office of Child Support Enforcement
    Ms. Sandra K. Gilmore, Director
    Department of Welfare
    1900 Washington Street, East
    Charleston, West Virginia 25305
    (304) 348-3780

WISCONSIN

Bureau of Child Support
    Mr. Duane Campbell, Director
    Division of Economic Assistance
    18 South Thornton Avenue
    Madison, Wisconsin 53708
    (608) 266-0528

Children's Rights Inc. of Wisconsin
    Edith St. John, President
    121 Elliot St.
    Tanesville, Wisconsin 53545
    (608) 752-8789

WYOMING

Child Support Enforcement Section
    Mrs. Shirley Kingston, Director
    Division of Public Assistance & Social Services
    State Department of Health and Social Service
    Hathaway Building
    Cheyenne, Wyoming 82002
    (307) 777-6083

CHAPTER XIII

AN AFTERWORD

*More money is being spent to care for stray dogs
than to find missing children.*

*John Walsh
Father of Adam Walsh*

A TIME FOR CHANGE

If more parents were more careful about their children, about where and with whom they play, about who cares for them, who their coaches, teachers, and adult friends are, there would be fewer cases of molestation, less opportunity for the sexually depraved to prey on them.

If we loved them more, listened to them more, fewer would run away. If our government officials recognized basic family financial support as a necessity rather than a privilege or reward, we would not have so many throwaways. We could return more runaways if our national budget provided more for runaway shelters and crisis hotlines and intervention.

Fewer madmen would victimize children if we made the punishment fit the crime.

Lost children would be recovered sooner if more programs were made available for recovery and training for law enforcement personnel in handling the problem.

More children would return if the press exercised both generosity and prudence: generosity with newspaper space and TV time, prudence with sensationalization of child abduction and murder.

We must start somewhere. At home is a good place.

The children pictured on the following pages are still missing. We hope that you or someone you know will be able to identify them so that they can soon be reunited with their families and loved ones.

Two million children vanish every year. To discover a child missing is probably one of the grimmest realizations a parent can make.

CHILD SAFE PRODUCTS decided it wanted to do something about the national tragedy of child abductions, runaways, parental kidnappings, and sexual abuse. Through extensive research CHILD SAFE PRODUCTS discovered that very little educational material dealing with these subjects was available to parents, children, and schools.

So, CHILD SAFE PRODUCTS developed a Child Safe program designed to create a safer environment to help children recognize — without frightening them — that there are bad people "out there" who may wish to harm them.

Each program for children deals with a specific skill that a child can use to minimize the chances of his being harmed. The programs are presented in a way that is entertaining so a child will remain interested while he is learning.

Programs and materials for parents were designed to help adults recognize some of the people, places, and situations that can put their child at risk and to offer guidelines for prevention and recovery.

It is the hope of CHILD SAFE PRODUCTS that these educational materials will make America once again a safe place for our children.

BOOKS

1) **My Child Is Not Missing** — A Parent's Guide Book — A comprehensive resource book for parents (and teachers) about prevention and molestation and a step-by-step recovery system for missing children (runaways, parental kidnappings, criminal abductions), illustrated trade softback $12.95

2) **Why Kids Leave Home** — A book that explains to parents and interested adults why children leave home voluntarily. Based on extensive research, the text discusses the breakdown of the family and how it has contributed to the numbers of young people who turn to cults and pedophiles for acceptance. Information is also given about prevention and legislation that will help those trying to recover a runaway, trade softback $12.95, hardcover $16.95

3) **Child Pac Data Cards™:** A highly detailed information and identification file on your child, containing items of vital importance: fingerprints, photos, body charts, dental records, hair and fingernail analysis samples, handwriting examples, school information, etc., which will assist you and the authorities in the quick recovery of your missing child. Spiral bound, $9.95

4) **Child Safe Products' Missing Child Directory:** A compilation of almost 600 organizations, national, state and local, both profit and non-profit all designed to help parents and children with kidnappings, sexual abuse and other related problems. The directory lists all the organizations by state, has the name of the contact person and a description of each agency's services.

SAFE 'N SOUND™ AUDIO LIBRARY

Educational and entertaining audio cassette tapes for children and parents which make the listener aware of the situations in which abduction and molestation most frequently occur and how to deal with them.

SAFE 'N SOUND™ AUDIO LIBRARY FOR AGES 5 TO 8

Program #1: MY BODY'S MY OWN
A program that teaches a young child the privacy of his body and his need to speak up if it is violated. $9.95

Program #2: THE EMERGENCY
A program that teaches your child the importance of knowing how to use a pay telephone to handle an emergency. $9.95

Program #3: ALONE IN THE CAR
A program that teaches your child the dangers of being alone in a car. $9.95

Program #4: ALONE IN THE CROWD
A program that teaches your child to recognize common lures of child abductors in a shopping mall. $9.95

Program #5: THE PASSWORD
A program that teaches your child to recognize a common lure of child abductors and the importance of a family code word to elude the child-snatch. $9.95

Program #6: ALONE AT HOME
A program that teaches your child how to respond to various situations when he is left home alone. $9.95

Program #7: THE EMPTY HOUSE
A program that teaches your child about the risks of playing in an empty field or house. $9.95

Program #8: "I'M LOST"
A program that teaches your child how to find help if he is lost. $9.95

Program #9: HELPING A STRANGER
A program that explains how child abductors enlist the aid of children in finding a supposedly missing pet. $9.95

Program #10: DON'T HURT ME
A program that familiarizes your child with the steps he can take if he is abused and his right to be free from physical abuse. $9.95

Program #11: "DO YOU WANT A RIDE?"
A program that teaches a child to avoid another common lure of the childnapper: an offer to help. $9.95

Program #12: "WHERE ARE WE GOING, DADDY?"
A program that teaches a child when and how to say no to a parent or adult who is trying to abduct him. $9.95

SAFE 'N SOUND™ AUDIO LIBRARY FOR AGES 9 TO 13

Program #1:   PRIVATE PARTS
A program that teaches an older child about the privacy of his body and his need to speak up if it is violated. $9.95

Program #2:   THE STRANGER'S INVITATION
A program that teaches your child about the dangers of accepting offers of employment from strangers. $9.95

Program #3:   THE STRANGER'S HOUSE
A program that teaches your child to recognize the dangers of going to a stranger's house alone. $9.95

Program #4:   THE RUNAWAY
A program that teaches your child that running away is not a solution to his problem. $9.95

Program #5:   CULTS: ARE THEY THE ANSWER?
A program that teaches your child to recognize cult propaganda and to avoid it. $9.95

Program #6:   DRUGS: ARE THEY THE ANSWER?
A program that teaches your child to recognize a drug pusher's "sales pitch" and how to counter it. $9.95

Program #7:   THE BUDDY SYSTEM
A program that teaches your child to use the "buddy system" whenever he is in a public area or without adult supervision. $9.95

Program #8:   THUMBING A RIDE
A program that teaches your child about the dangers of hitch-hiking. $9.95

Program #9:   THE STRANGER'S OFFER
A program that teaches your child to recognize one of the common lures of child abductors: the promise of money and gifts. $9.95

Program #10:   "YOUR MOTHER SENT ME"
A program that teaches your child to recognize one of the common lures of child abductors: the reference to family members. $9.95

Program #11:   "CAN YOU HELP ME?"
A program that teaches your child to recognize another common lure of childnappers: the request for help. $9.95

Program #12:   "MAY I COME IN?"
A program that alerts your child to the potential dangers of allowing strangers into his home. $9.95

SAFE 'N SOUND™ AUDIO LIBRARY FOR PARENTS AND ADULTS

Program #1: THE CHILD ABDUCTOR: A PROFILE
A program which alerts parents to the problems of child abduction and describes the individuals who may be kidnappers. $9.95

Program #2: CHILD ABDUCTION: PREVENTION
A program which describes parental guidelines for keeping a child safe from abductors. $9.95

Program #3: "MY CHILD IS MISSING!": RECOVERY
A step-by-step program to assist parents should their child become missing. $9.95

Program #4: HOME ALONE
A program to help parents who must occasionally leave their child at home alone. $9.95

Program #5: THE CHILD MOLESTOR
A program which alerts parents to the problem of sexual abuse, describes the types of sexual offenders, and offers guidelines for protecting a child. $9.95

Program #6: SEXUAL ABUSE: THE WARNING SIGNS
A program which alerts parents to signs that their child is being abused and offers guidelines for action. $9.95

Program #7: PARENTAL KIDNAPPING: PREVENTION
A program which alerts the parent to the problem of parental kidnapping and offers guidelines for keeping a child safe from this type of abduction. $9.95

Program #8: PARENTAL KIDNAPPING: RECOVERY
A step-by-step program and a description of the laws that will assist a parent in recovering a child abducted by a spouse or relative. $9.95

Program #9: THE RUNAWAY: PREVENTION AND RECOVERY
A program which alerts the parent to the signals children often give before they run away and offers guidelines for prevention and recovery. $9.95

Program #10: CHOOSING A DAYCARE CENTER AND BABYSITTER
A program which offers guidelines to parents for choosing a day care center or a babysitter and assigning her responsibility for the safety of the child and the home. $9.95

Program #11: TEACHING YOUR CHILD ASSERTIVENESS
A program which demonstrates how a parent can teach his child assertiveness skills in order to avoid abduction and other potentially dangerous situations. $9.95

Program #12: CHILD ABUSE: THE BREAKING POINT
A program that alerts the concerned parent to recognize the situations which may cause him to be abusive and that offers guidelines for prevention and treatment of child abuse. $9.95

PARENT'S ACTION PROGRAM

The Parent's Action Program is a complete package for prevention and recovery of missing children. The package includes: Child Safe Products' book, MY CHILD IS NOT MISSING, the first comprehensive resource book about prevention of child abduction and molestation with a step-by-step recovery system for missing children. Also included in the package is THE PARENT'S ACTION PLAN, a pre-planned methodical search system which helps to avoid the confusion and memory lapses which occur and cost precious time when it counts most — when a child is missing.

Another item included in the Parent's Action Program is the CHILD PAC DATA CARDS, a highly detailed information and identification file on the child, containing items of vital importance: fingerprints, photos, body charts, dental records, hair and fingernail analysis samples, handwriting examples, school information, etc., all of which will assist parents and authorities in the quick recovery of a missing child.

The child's Voice Audio Recording is the final feature of the Parent's Action Program. The tape will allow authorities to identify the child and move quickly to return the child to his or her parents.

PACKAGE PRICE
$29.95

BREAK AWAY/GET AWAY — A quick but thorough VIDEO TAPE COURSE designed by a nationally recognized self defense consultant to law enforcement agencies. The course is divided into nine lessons, which can be shown individually or in combinations. Each lesson shows a different technique, including twists, turns, kicks, and other preventative methods which will let children elude an abductor. The lessons are entertaining, which means the children will learn without becoming frightened. This video program can equip your child in a few hours with the practical training to escape most would-be kidnappers and molesters.

For more information call Child Safe Products, Inc. (305) 472-6070 (Florida) — 1 (800) 334-0090 (Toll-Free Outside Florida).

To order additional items from Child Safe Products, Inc. send the price indicated plus $2.00 for postage and handling (Florida residents add 5% sales tax) to:

Child Safe Products, Inc.
Publishing Division
449 North University Drive
Plantation, Florida 33324

Materials are available at special quantity discounts for bulk purchases, sales promotions, premiums or fund raising. Special book or book excerpts can also be created to fit specific needs. Call or write the office of the publisher for complete details.
